18 INSIGHTS ON LiFe

for Contemporary Times from the Gita

ANAND MEHROTRA

INDIA • SINGAPORE • MALAYSIA

Copyright © Anand Mehrotra 2023
All Rights Reserved.

ISBN 978-81-939882-5-1

This book has been published with all efforts taken to make the material error-free after the consent of the author. However, the author and the publisher do not assume and hereby disclaim any liability to any party for any loss, damage, or disruption caused by errors or omissions, whether such errors or omissions result from negligence, accident, or any other cause.

While every effort has been made to avoid any mistake or omission, this publication is being sold on the condition and understanding that neither the author nor the publishers or printers would be liable in any manner to any person by reason of any mistake or omission in this publication or for any action taken or omitted to be taken or advice rendered or accepted on the basis of this work. For any defect in printing or binding the publishers will be liable only to replace the defective copy by another copy of this work then available.

Also by Anand Mehrotra

This Is That
Patanjali's Yoga Sutras, Padas 1 and 2

That Is This
Patanjali's Yoga Sutras, Padas 3 and 4

Liberation
An Interpretation of Isha Upanishad

For

All the Discoverers

on the

Journey of Self-Realisation

Contents

Introduction		*9*
A Brief History		*11*
Lesson 1	On Taking Responsibility	25
Lesson 2	On Mastering the Mind	34
Lesson 3	On Skill in Action	48
Lesson 4	On Knowledge Leading to Bliss	63
Lesson 5	On Letting Go	87
Lesson 6	On Inner Unity	103
Lesson 7	On Realising the Self	111
Lesson 8	On a Life of Love	119
Lesson 9	On Unlocking the Secrets Within	131
Lesson 10	On Discovering the Excellent	142
Lesson 11	On Seeing and Believing	149
Lesson 12	On Realising Love and Gaining Connection	158

Lesson 13	On the Distinction between the Knower and the Known	166
Lesson 14	On the Three Vibrational States of the Leela	175
Lesson 15	On Climbing the Tree of Life	183
Lesson 16	On Cultivating Qualities of Conscious Growth	192
Lesson 17	On Moving from Faith to Knowing	204
Lesson 18	On Understanding the Meaning through Knowing the Meaninglessness	207

About the Author   *219*

Introduction

In the Yog-Vedantic tradition, the Scriptures, the teachings, are in codes. So there has been a long, living tradition of discussion and exploration. That is what has kept the timeless yogic teachings alive and relevant without particular dharma, without any particular organisation pushing the agenda, without any forcible conversions. Anyone who comes to the spiritual path ultimately comes through their own volition, not forced, not coerced into it. So when you are on the spiritual path and you come to it, you come to it from something deep inside you. That is why these teachings will always be relevant, always are.

All the Sanskrit scriptures are written in code. They have to be deciphered. There has to be discussion and contemplation, expanding the truth which is inherent in the scriptures. That is why you can be reading different interpretations and they can all have different meanings.

That is what keeps the approach alive, actually. And it is celebrated. The exploration in this tradition is not frowned upon, unlike in some traditions where the word is fixed. One has to realise that the word, whether written or spoken, cannot be fixed. All meanings are dynamic. Krishna said that a fixed mind which is not dynamic, understanding which is not dynamic, knowing which is not deepening and getting to a deeper level of knowingness, is not knowing at all. The sattvic level of knowing maintains a level of dynamism. And it refines and understands.

– Anand Mehrotra

It was in this spirit of the Himalayan Yog-Vedantic Tradition that we heard the Bhagavad Gita interpreted in a magnificent, brilliant, comprehensive manner by living Master Yogi, Anand Mehrotra, a contemporary Himalayan Rishi.

Anand channelled the Sattva Yoga Academy course on the fundamental evolution of being, on how to move in the direction of Light. He led the students to dive deep to explore the most important and relevant teachings of the Bhagavad Gita's 18 chapters. They discovered how these teachings will upgrade their lives to a whole new level. The interpretation given enabled us to gain new perspectives on the nature of reality.

A Brief History

The Bhagavad Gita is the path to liberation and is contained within the Mahabharata. One of the best known of the Indian scriptures, it is not only the scripture of the yogi but one of the greatest sources of spiritual wisdom, as relevant now as when it was first heard, for no matter what is occurring in life, the teachings of yoga are always relevant. There are numerous Gitas but the most revered is the Bhagavad Gita because it contains the essence of all the Vedic wisdom. These are timeless teachings, as relevant now as when they were first heard because no matter how big the challenge seems, liberation is always possible.

The name Mahabharata refers to its grand scale, an epic story of an Indian dynasty with a multitude of characters exploring different psychological aspects of human nature. Intricately woven and phenomenally deep, it is profound in its implications and scope. You see, it is really dealing with humanity as a whole as the story of humanity is a story of conflict; conflict being a uniquely human experience. The extent of conflict within the human psyche, within the human being, is far greater than in any other species on the face of this planet. We humans have the ability to make choices, to ask questions, and wherever there is choice there is going to be a certain level of conflict. Whereas the cow is simply a cow, effortlessly existing with no real choice-making required in life. Of course, on an existential level there are certain choices that the cow makes but at the grander level the cow remains a cow doing what a cow does, innocent and oblivious to the other possibilities of existence. The human being on the other hand cannot remain as such. So the whole conflict within the Mahabharata is really an exploration of what it is to be human. Conflict only arises at the level of the ego-mind; it cannot be achieved at a higher level. For to truly resolve conflict, it is not about finding a solution at the level where the conflict arose but rather by elevating the consciousness state to that level where the conflict dissolves.

Where did the Mahabharata come from? Created by Vyasa, it is the longest poetic piece in the ancient world and the Bhagavad Gita, set within it, is the jewel in this crown of spiritual wisdom. This Song Celestial is written in such a way as to be melodic and simple to chant, designed to be memorized, remembered and shared. And even though this conversation that is the Bhagavad Gita is between Arjuna and Krishna who both inhabit masculine bodies, the teaching itself is from the Divine Mother and the nature of this mother is to nurture you, to liberate you, to love you. It is the mother that feeds you, grows you, brings you forth. Anything that exists in shape and form ultimately comes through the mother and this wisdom comes from the Divine Mother, moving through Krishna. That is the great brilliance of this teaching; it has the potential to nourish you, to transform you, to birth you into higher and higher states of consciousness. You come out of the Gita anew, rebirthed. But one must understand that Krishna is not a linear teacher and yoga is not a linear teaching and that these profound teachings have to be taken as a whole.

The scriptures associated with Vyasa are voluminous and the sheer amount suggests it is unlikely that Vyasa was a single person but rather a consciousness state inhabited by different individuals. It was not created from a place of thought but instead the wisdom flowed, it was channelled. So this Song Celestial flowed through Vyasa and the understanding of this knowledge is not reached through thought but rather it spontaneously occurs at a particular state of consciousness. In the context of linear time, it is the Vedas followed by the Upanishads, the Tantras, the Sutras and then the Puranas, in which we find the Mahabharata. When the Yog-Vedantic teachings reached this level, the wisdom needed a narrative, a setting and characters to entertain and engage the listener fully. The people were not really practicing these teachings, not living them. Vedic science is not just to be listened to or read, it is to be experienced. Putting the wisdom into a narrative was giving people an example of how to live it.

In this manner, the teachings started to be delivered in a unique and exciting way to engage the audience. The Bhagavad Gita's setting in a battle is exciting and captivated imaginations. It has everything going on: the battlefield, family conflict, the hero in crisis facing his greatest challenge, and it all flows as a song. That is why this is such an extraordinary teaching, set on the battlefield yet shared as a song. There is an intensity to the story juxtaposed with the softness and ease of the manner in which it is being relayed. So when we enter this book, it is not with a dry intellect but rather with the heart and mind unified. For poetry is not to be understood and appreciated by a dry intellect; poetry arises from the heart and is felt in the heart. The song arises from the feminine part of who we are, the conflict from the masculine. To fully comprehend this wisdom, we must enter this teaching through the heart and the mind together. We must enter it with great reverence, great devotion and at the same time with a sharp intellect. We must be alert and aware because it contains the nectar of all the Vedic and Upanishadic teachings in such a very concise and beautiful manner. This is such a vast, comprehensive set of teachings; it is wisdom that fundamentally addresses the evolution of being.

In an historical context, Kurukshetra is still very much in existence in the north of India, between Delhi and Punjab. But despite being set in a very real time and place, it is important to realise that the Mahabharata itself is fundamentally a teaching tool, as all Sanskrit scriptures are. They are scriptures of wisdom, of vidya, of knowledge; knowledge that is both elevating and liberating. None are just stories told for the sake of entertainment; all are told to really transform the person who is interacting with them. So in this Song Celestial, Krishna is giving his teachings on the battlefield not in an ashram, not in a temple, not on a beach. Vyasa placed this story on the battlefield for a reason. On this battlefield are Arjuna's teachers, his cousins, people he has loved, grown up and played with, so he is facing an immense level of pain. The magnitude of this challenge shows the listener that there can be no crisis too big in their own life where these teachings will not be relevant. There is no crisis big enough which you cannot transcend through your awareness, through your wisdom. When you dive deep into the ocean of wisdom within yourself, then you can transcend and rise up to such an incredible level. Setting the Gita on the battlefield reminds us that these battles rage on within communities, within families, within countries, within every individual. The only way out of such conflict is not by remaining the same but rather it is through elevating one's own status, transcending that consciousness state within which conflict is born and conflict is experienced. The Gita shares all this with us on both the level of the intellect and on the level of the heart; if we really dive deep, we will come out victorious.

The Mahabharata is made up of eighteen books, eighteen voluminous parvas, and within that the Bhagavad Gita also has eighteen chapters. It is so beautiful already, just to see the harmony of numbers here. Eighteen representing the trinity of trinity, nine. It is really referring to cosmic design because from the yogic perspective, nine is the number of totality. The Bhagavad Gita is within the sixth book of the Mahabharata, the Bhishma Parva, and the battle that it describes is fought over eighteen days by eighteen armies. There are four speakers in the Gita: Krishna, the great Master, the Avatar, the bringer of the purest teaching; Arjuna, the great disciple, the Atman, the yogi; Sanjaya who is listening and relaying the teachings and through whom we are really able to get a window into the discourse, and Dhritarashtra who is the blind king, the ego-mind, listening to Sanjaya report what is happening. Within the eighteen chapters of the Gita, there are seven hundred verses representing the seven chakras; Krishna speaks in 574, Arjuna has 84, Sanjaya has 41 and Dhritarashtra only one.

As with all the ancient Yog-Vedantic teachings, the access points to the Gita are numerous with layer upon layer of meaning. Many, many commentaries have been written and each time you read one you will find a very distinct interpretation. That is the fundamental nature of all Sanskrit scriptures; they are designed to be interpreted from different consciousness states. These scriptures are not dead; they are living traditions and that is their great beauty. There is no one translation or interpretation of these teachings which is the ultimate authority. Different teachers access this wisdom from different consciousness states and so bring forth different expressions of the same teachings. The conversation in the Gita is between the teacher and the student. When you dive deep into it you will bring forth the teaching most relevant for you at that time.

The main characters are Arjuna and Krishna, the student and the teacher, and we see this incredible relationship building up between them; there is an immense bond there. Often Krishna speaks of Arjuna as a beloved friend but at the same time Arjuna knows that Krishna is not just his friend, he is also his great Master and he never forgets that. What drives this relationship is this immense love and reverence, Krishna's love for Arjuna and Arjuna's love for Krishna. We see this clearly as the battle commences between Arjuna, commanding the Pandavas, and his cousin, Duryodhana, with the Kauravas. Duryodhana is abundant in incorrect knowledge and is the head of the Kauravas; Arjuna is the middle brother of the five Pandava boys and within the chakra system represents the Manipura. As the story goes, the Kauravas and the Pandavas are at war and so Duryodhana and Arjuna, both seeking help to vanquish their enemy, turn to Krishna for aid but when they reach Lord Krishna, they find him sleeping. Duryodhana sits down right by Krishna's head, above him due to his ego and arrogance. When Arjuna enters the chamber, he places himself at the feet of Krishna, due to his love and reverence for his Lord. They remain there quietly waiting while he sleeps but as Krishna awakes, his eyes fall upon Arjuna first because he is sitting at his feet. He welcomes him and then asks them both why they have come, even though he is Krishna and knows all things because one has to engage on the human level to keep the story going. Otherwise, if you remain at the level of transcendent knowing, there can be no tale to tell. So Krishna asks the question and both Arjuna and Duryodhana explain that they are there to seek his help on the battlefield. Krishna spontaneously answers that he will serve both men but they have to make a choice. One side can have Krishna's mighty army and the other side can have only Krishna himself but he will not take up weapons or engage in any level of conflict. Now Krishna commanded one of the greatest armies of all time so whoever made that choice would have it at their disposal but whoever chose him would only get him. Since he saw Arjuna first, he asks him to choose and without hesitation, no thought, no doubt in his mind for even a moment, Arjuna chooses Krishna. Duryodhana is supremely joyous about this because he wants the mighty army; now he feels absolutely certain of victory. But Arjuna is blissfully content because he gets to be with his beloved Krishna. So they are both very happy with this outcome.

We can see that this is the classic story set up already, a tale that plays out over and over and over again. In the beginning that which is not in alignment always seems to be the more powerful. It looks like Duryodhana and his mighty army are going to win this battle but when you expand your vision, you will eventually see that it is dharma, the divine law, that is victorious. In all good storylines, eventually light will prevail over darkness, that is the fundamental law of nature. If you can't find dharma prevailing, you just need to expand your slice of now. A hero will always start with great opposition and it is the transcendence of that opposition that brings out the best in them. That is the classic hero's journey and it does not just play out in mythical realms on a faraway battlefield; it actually plays out in our own lives too. So now we start with this incredible relationship between Arjuna and Krishna; Arjuna, the greatest of the warriors, Krishna, the wisest of the wise and together they stand against Duryodhana and his mighty army. Arjuna asks Krishna to be his charioteer as they prepare for the battle, so Krishna drives the five horses while Arjuna rides in the chariot. Here we see the five horses symbolising the five senses, Arjuna is the soul, the Atman, totally surrendered to

Krishna, the Cosmic Being, and when the soul unites with the Cosmic Being, invincibility is gained. All wisdom is naturally derived from that place. All supreme knowledge, all great intelligence, comes from the Cosmic Being.

But there is more in this brilliant discourse because in the Bhagavad Gita there are actually two conversations going on simultaneously. One is between Arjuna and Krishna and the other is between Dhritarashtra, the blind king and father of Duryodhana and all the Kauravas, and Sanjaya, the clairvoyant with infinite sight. Dhritarashtra has the opening question to get the ball rolling; concerned about the battle, he asks Sanjaya, what does he see? Sanjaya will then explain what is happening. So what we are listening to in the Bhagavad Gita is actually what is being relayed through Sanjaya to Dhritarashtra. It's like the original internet, Sanjaya is live streaming, reporting in real time. There is a great irony in this set up and that is the genius of Vyasa; Sanjaya, the seer of all, is speaking to the blind king, the one who cannot see, and he is also speaking to us. By putting Sanjaya there, Vyasa removes himself from the narrative; so when we read the Gita, we get a clear view directly into the discourse between Arjuna and Krishna as if we are right there too and we can become truly absorbed in the consciousness state of Krishna.

In using these two separate conversations to tell this story, we can quite clearly see the different effect this knowledge, this wisdom that is being poured out, is having on the different receivers. Dhritarashtra is listening to the exact same thing as Arjuna but by the end Arjuna has gained a level of invincibility, all his ignorance is destroyed and he is victorious but Dhritarashtra's condition only worsens. Listening to the same wisdom, one gains liberation and the other does not, he regresses. This is Vyasa giving us a choice. That is the beauty of all the Vedic scriptures; they are not sermons, they are invitations. You always have a choice: you can either dive deep into the Gita like Arjuna or be like Dhritarashtra, the blind king, and just sit there passively. The knowledge is available to all equally. Vyasa is very clear, it is not the knowledge which creates the transformation, it is how the receiver receives the knowledge. It is the level of consciousness, the level of engagement that the student is at, that really creates the magic. We can choose to accept the invitation to transcend the Dhritarashtra nature within us, the ego-mind, or we can decline it and remain blind. Dhritarashtra is not interested in the opportunity to evolve. He only wants to find out what is happening to his children and after his one question he does not ask anything else. Even though he is listening to all that wisdom that Krishna is sharing, he is not interested in it. So the end result is Arjuna's liberation and Dhritarashtra's destruction.

A question is a precursor to the answer; the questions you ask yourself are a clue into your consciousness state. Whatever those questions you are asking yourself are, your mind will start to look for those answers. Our lives become the answer to those questions that we ask; to affect change and growth we must look at what questions we are asking. Arjuna is asking his questions not from a place of challenge but from a place of deep, reverent inquiry. The Bhagavad Gita is a discussion between Master and student; they have a shared intention of getting not only into a state of great unity together but also of elevating individually. By the end of the conversation the solution is already being experienced by the one who asked the questions. It is important for us to realise that this is a dialogue not a monologue. It is not a sermon. The Gita is not asking you to believe in something. Questions are being asked, doubts are being cleared, contradictions resolved. These teachings are to be understood and applied, not just believed in. This is a discussion between a student and a Master with a shared relationship of love, not of fear.

Arjuna knows of Krishna's great love for him but he always reveres him as his teacher. That is such an important aspect in understanding this. And at the end, after answering all these questions in the most eloquent manner, offering the most profound teaching, Krishna gives Arjuna a choice, so it is now up to him how he responds. He can do what he feels is right to do. He must decide and whatever he chooses to do, Krishna says, he will support him. This is the brilliance of the Bhagavad Gita. For it is you who decides, you who makes the choice, and the universe organises itself around the choices you make. No one can do it for you. There is no one out there who can fix your problems if you just pray hard enough. Teachings are available, technology is available. But whatever you begin to consistently align yourself with, that is what will ultimately be delivered to you. We live in a self-validating system; the universe will validate whatever consciousness state you most consistently maintain. Krishna shares all these teachings of the Divine with Arjuna but he still makes him aware of his own responsibility.

Arjuna, the great warrior archer, the recipient of this wisdom, has been consistent in his devotion and his practice so he has already gained a certain level of deserving power to be able to absorb these teachings of Krishna. But even Arjuna can feel challenged and despondent. The Bhagavad Gita starts with the challenge that he is about to face so what we are learning here is that whenever you are challenged or feel overwhelmed, if you apply this wisdom, you will be liberated. When you bring out the wisdom within you, when you dive deep into your own transcendental level of being, you will prevail. Enlightenment is not the end game. Enlightenment is the ever-increasing revelation of light and this first chapter in the Gita is a testimony to that. Arjuna knows that even in this time of despondency, he can surrender into his heart and be open to the supreme wisdom.

Krishna is the one who knows all. Within the Mahabharata, Krishna is addressed on the historic level as a great leader, a king who faces challenges and opposition. In the Bhagavad Gita, Krishna is revealed on a whole different level. He becomes an expression of total unity, the voice of the pure Being. The Gita represents a discussion between you and your higher Self, a conversation between the individualized soul and the indivisible Cosmic Soul, the finite expression speaking to infinite. So the beauty of this is, it starts from love, the eternal love affair that goes on within each and every one of us. For the finite is the infinite, the infinite is the finite.

The wave is the ocean, the ocean is the wave. Arjuna is the soul, Krishna is the Cosmic Soul. So as you enter the Bhagavad Gita, enter as Arjuna, aware of your own Dhritarashtra nature and with the intention of raising yourself up.

There is nothing escapist about the teachings of yoga. Everyone in the Mahabharata is fully engaged in life and no one in the Gita is running away. This is about being here, evolving here, not escaping from here. When one is born into this body, expressing as this body, there is going to be conflict that one will have to face. The conflict is not a curse; it is the gift of being human. It is only due to incorrect understanding when one is not awake that the conflict becomes a curse. If one aligns to the state of Arjuna within oneself when one faces conflict, illumination is gained. When one remains as Dhritarashtra, then only suffering is experienced. In the relative field of reality, conflict is going to be there no matter who you are. In life you will always face a certain level of challenge but ultimately all conflict that you face is the inadequacy of the self. That is the fundamental root of all problems, the inadequacy of the self. So Krishna speaks to Arjuna and elevates the self from the inadequate self to a greater integrated Self. As the status of the self evolves, the problems dissolve. A challenge is only turned into a crisis, into suffering, within the consciousness state of the inadequate self.

The brilliance of these teachings is over 18 chapters, in 700 verses; pure elegance, this beauty in motion. The supreme skill in action. The mastery of Krishna, of Vyasa, is that the Bhagavad Gita is both remembered and heard and so this scripture has a unique position within the comprehensive Yog-Vedantic teachings. As part of the

Mahabharata, it has an historical context; it is part of this vast story that was at that time first spoken and then remembered. And it is simultaneously heard within from that place of deep meditation. This is teaching received directly from the source and so it doesn't matter when in linear time we think it was written down; the relevance of this incredible wisdom remains irrespective of what time it is written because it is always explored in the now. For anything to be truly liberating, it has to be relevant now, applicable now. The incredible value of the teachings in the Gita is that it is simultaneously philosophy of the truth and the science of being, art and science together. It appeals to the heart and to the intellect.

So as you read this interpretation of the Bhagavad Gita, the way to truly access this knowledge, to fully realise the lessons within, is not at the level of thought but rather at the level of soul. To experience it is to awaken to a deeper level of knowing, to establish oneself at a deeper level of being. So dive deep within your heart. Activate the Arjuna within. Align yourself with Arjuna. Allow the Gita, the Divine Mother flowing through Krishna, the celestial teacher, to flow into you and wipe out all conditioning, all imprints from the past. Realise within your heart, within your own awareness, the possibility of expanding your own divine, deserving nature. Know that the presence of conflict is not a sign of weakness but rather the gift of being human. Align yourself to this truth and you will find great strength. For in this lies opportunity, from chaos emerges greater order. This is an opportunity for each and every one of us to rise up into our true nature, for wherever this occurs there is winning energy.

Lesson 1
On Taking Responsibility

We can all understand despondency and disillusionment. When we have been challenged and have felt lost, beaten down by events, we have all faced that in our lives at times. So we can identify with those feelings but unity can arise from that place. Anyone who is going through any level of awakening is going to experience this despondency, face this doubt. As you begin to awaken, you will find you have a greater capacity to see and from that place a certain level of sadness can appear in the beginning stages, whereas those who have no introspection whatsoever bask in this false sense of arrogance. As the law goes, the greater the ignorance, the greater the arrogance. The arrogance, this confidence, is false. It is insecurity masquerading as confidence. We have all seen this, the more ignorant someone is, the louder they seem to be shouting.

When we are blind on the level of awareness, attached to the ego-mind, we become the designers of our own undoing, blind to our self-destructive behaviour. Instead of elevating our consciousness state, we stoop down to a lower level, are drawn to co-dependent relationships where one is feeding the other ignorance instead of elevating one another. Relationships based on passive co-dependency are feeding on each other's unconscious attachments. When the individuals who are in the state of ignorance, dominated by the ego-mind and the lower tendencies, find one negative thought, they can reproduce that into hundreds of negative thoughts very quickly. Each and every one of us has had that experience when we find ourselves dominated by incorrect knowledge. As soon as we get an attachment to a toxic thought, it starts to multiply a hundred-fold. Mysteriously, for some reason we find it takes us much longer to adopt progressive habits, evolutionary behaviours from which we will benefit. Whereas the negative tendencies expand much quicker, grow, take root and multiply, both individually and culturally.

The one stuck in their victimhood can only witness their own destruction for that confirms their identity. The victim has to confirm their victim identity by exposing themselves to a scenario where they are helpless and can watch the destruction being created before them. One can always make a change but many choose to remain passive and stay in their victim identity, blind to joy. If we choose to remain in the ego-mind state instead of engaging in an elevated evolutionary manner, we are just feeding off our co-dependency and so remain the same. This decision, if left uncorrected, sets a sequence in motion for a life dominated by attachment, blind to the truth and our unlived potential. Those identified with the ego-mind don't move on from their victim identity and remain stuck. We must understand that everything in one's life is the way it is because one gives it permission to be so. If you sow the seeds of an apple, then to expect a mango tree to grow would go against the laws of nature; as you sow, so shall you reap. Sowing is always in the present moment; all your seeds are planted in the present moment. Think carefully about what seeds you are sowing in the present moment.

When one begins to awaken, there is a certain level of fluctuation that occurs. We can all identify with these uncertainties; they are the fluctuations of the mind. The certainty born from ignorant arrogance is not a certainty that leads one to invincibility. This is a certainty which leads down a path of destruction; absolute destruction. One of the greatest obstacles to knowledge is knowledge when that knowledge is incorrect. Always remain open and interested, you will be well served if you are interested in gaining wisdom instead of just being right. Avoid a closed mind, interested only in being right, not being wise and designing suffering at an elevated rate for oneself and one's fellow beings. Unfortunately, this overconfidence, this fanatic zeal, is very seductive. People get sucked into it. This is false power, the perverted vision of power. For these beings to be powerful, others have to be weak. For them to be abundant, others have to be poor. For them to be respected, others have to be disrespected. This is a state of constant conflict. We all know people who can only make themselves look good and feel good by putting others down. It is not about what they have achieved but what others have not. But remember, the ignorant don't know that they are ignorant. Ignorance with the awareness that there is ignorance is not ignorant; that is the beginning of wisdom. But ignorance without the awareness, that is dangerous. That is what creates destruction.

We see this now, we see it play out in the world of politics, in the economic arenas. We see it play out over and over and over again. A person with a hyperactive ego starts to generate a certain level of intensity and as this intensity increases, people who are not on the path of progression, who are not awakening within themselves, naturally become seduced through the propaganda. People are drawn to propaganda because they do not know how to think for themselves. They have not developed a level of introspection, they let others do the thinking for them, create ideas for them, choose the path for them. But when you go within and start to awaken, you will find, as you step out of the cave of your own conditioning, that you will feel a little bit insecure, less sure. You will feel less sure than the one who has no introspection whatsoever, who has totally given up sovereignty over their thoughts and has fallen into the conditioning because there is a natural tendency in the denser consciousness state to be more confident, to be more certain, to be more committed to a cause than the one who is awakening. It is just a fluctuation that is going on as one is stepping out of the dark and is not fully in the light yet. So remember, with great arrogance comes great ignorance. Humility and wisdom go hand in hand and ignorance and arrogance go hand in hand, individually, culturally and collectively.

In the absence of introspection, of a contemplative culture and a tradition of wisdom, the hyperactive ego will dominate and will suck in all those who are not developing their own personal culture. Destruction by association. It doesn't matter how much the ego-mind accumulates, it forever remains tormented. It doesn't matter what you accumulate because the state of bliss is not a state of accumulation, the state of abundance is not a state of acquisition. It is a state of consciousness. It is not about having or not having stuff which sets you free; your mind sets you free. It all comes from within. That is the law of nature. The laws of human beings are arbitrary and can be broken but this is the law of nature and cannot be broken.

For a change to occur within, one has to come to the point where one wants to see clearly. When one starts to awaken within oneself, one has to let go of one's identity, of who one thinks one is. That has to be faced. We have to be willing to face that without any fear of judgement, be unafraid to be vulnerable. So this disillusionment that occurs in the beginning is merely fluctuation. We are creating the crisis, this resistance to change, this resistance to grow, this resistance to expand because we are so used to attachments. This is a very clear lesson. When we start to awaken, we have to face all our stories, all our conditioned identities, our belief structures that we hold so dear; all our old habits and patterns show up within our own consciousness and they all have to be faced and let go. Even when seeking is sincere, we have to first face our own conditioning, our resistance, our attachments. We have to face our history. Emotions are subtler than intellect and thoughts go in the direction of emotions, so when we are moved emotionally, we start to generate more and more complex thinking. And when we are moved emotionally, if we are not alert and clear, the ego-mind starts to multiply these thoughts one after the other. Even though the point from where we start is correct, we soon begin to dig a hole for ourself. When we get into those states, we find that if we are not in charge of our emotions, if we are not emotionally intelligent, we cannot be intellectually intelligent. How one feels, so shall one think; our thoughts will go in the direction of our feelings.

Devotion, love that is surrendered, is the highest emotion that can make us emotionally healthy. Devotion elevates the status, then one can start to turn a crisis into an opportunity to learn. When one has reached that state where one is ready to receive the teachings, then one can learn, elevate and expand. So it is important for us to realise that at times we might feel weak, that we might feel uncertain, we might feel helpless in the world, helpless in the face of those with their hyperactive egos that are so certain of their point of view, screaming through loud speakers. But know this, as you align yourself to your true inner nature, as you awaken within your own cosmic consciousness, you gain invincibility. This arrogant, hyperactive ego ultimately only leads to destruction. The ignorant ones do not see the outcome of their actions and remain committed to their destruction. The wise are able to see the end in the beginning and so are able to correct the course. The wise can see the bigger picture; the ignorant remain with their narrow vision.

In the beginning, when one meditates one can see the thoughts. This appearance of thought is not because one has started to meditate; it is because one is now becoming aware. The mind always thinks a lot but, in the beginning, when one starts to meditate, one becomes aware of all these thoughts. As you become consistent in your practice, then the mind starts to locate that inner bliss, starts to get transcendent in its essential nature and the thoughts start to subside. When the mind is racing, spiralling, it is a classic example of what we all experience, this utter confusion. We believe that if we think more, we will get out of the confusion, we will un-confuse ourselves but it is the opposite; the excessive thought is causing the confusion. You can't come to clarity through excessive thought, it just doesn't happen. First one has to come to that level of deep silence within and then one is ready to listen; the despondency and disillusionment serves to exhaust our thoughts and bring us to that point of quiet surrender. Once we realise the limitation of our intellect, the limitation of our knowledge, then we are ready to shift.

As one often finds in life, before one can rise up, one has to hit rock bottom first. From crisis emerges brilliance, from chaos comes order, from destruction there is growth. That does not mean that all awakenings require despair but on a certain level that despondency, that despair, can be a precursor to illumination. When we commit to the path, we will have to face our resistance, face our conditioning, face our investments, face our shadows. Then, once we've weakened ourselves through overthinking, we can surrender and receive because irrespective of what state one gets oneself into, if one is in alignment then beauty can emerge. If you receive the knowledge and really awaken to your essential nature, then it is guaranteed that everything in your life will fall into place. All the challenges, all the dark nights, all those moments of feeling low, all those moments where you felt beaten, it will all fall into place when you are aligned with your essential nature. The requirement is only that you grow and awaken. If you do not grow, nothing falls into place. It all seems like a random assault on you and so the self remains forever inadequate, trying to escape and in the process creating suffering for itself, designing its own destruction.

The Absolute is the only thing that exists, so keep that in your field of awareness if you want to keep learning. Don't lose sight of the fundamental truth. Only through the correction of the intellect, through exposing oneself to higher knowledge, higher wisdom, can one find any relief from the conflict. Without that, there is no hope. You can accumulate everything but you will still lose. You can go live in the forest but you will still lose. You can try and run away but you will still lose. The only way to make sense of any of it is by elevating the status of self, by elevating the awareness, by elevating the consciousness state. And of course, it starts through elevating the status of the intellect, refining one's understanding. Without correct understanding, there is no correct thinking. Without correct thinking, there is no correct action. Incorrect understanding leads to incorrect thinking. Incorrect thinking leads to incorrect action. Incorrect action confirms the incorrect thinking, and then the cycle continues in the ever-repeating known. Incorrect knowledge, incorrect thinking, incorrect action, incorrect experience that confirms the incorrect knowledge. The self remains stuck in the ever-repeating known.

So remember as you go through life, there will often be times where you will find yourself in such despondency, in a state of fluctuation, but don't get into the spiral of thought. And when you do, pause, expose yourself to higher wisdom. Apply the technology and correct your inner state, get into that deep surrendered state and open yourself to higher wisdom, to the love of the Divine. Offer that which arises in you; offer it out instead of suppressing it and allow the wisdom to emerge within you. Awaken to a deeper level of knowing. Awaken to your own true nature. Have self-compassion for your own inherent weaknesses, your own inner resistance which might arise. Simultaneously, become available to transcendence, to growth, to the light of wisdom which will elevate your status. Surrender your fears, realise that the true strength of you lies in the silence of you.

Lesson 2
On Mastering the Mind

This is a teaching of the science of self-realisation; it is an open invitation to dive deep and discover this wisdom for yourself. At different times, different interpretations will arise, you will find different meanings because this is about the knowledge of Self. So one has to remain alert and aware as one dives deep because that is what is required if one is to evolve. To enter a transcendental level of consciousness, one needs to be refining the perception, refining the understanding, refining the intellect, for that is the method of dissecting and synthesizing wisdom. Honour the intellect and refine it; it's what creates a distinction between humans and other species. This intellect within the faculty of the mind is a powerful servant but a terrible master. So one must refine the perception to its finest level and dive deep to find the fundamental truth, going way beyond the surface, dissecting and then synthesizing, that is what this lesson teaches us. First we dissect and then we synthesize, dissect and synthesize, dissect and synthesize. If we only approach it in an abstract way, then we do not understand the finer values. If the soul, the true Self, does not refine and educate the intellect to move in the correct direction then the intellect, which is designed to find meaning, looks for it in the accumulations of the conditioned memory and makes up a false meaning. Then as the intellect generates this false meaning, we identify with it, take ownership of this false idea and make it part of the 'who I am' story. That is the mistaken identity which is at the root of all suffering in the human condition. It is very important for us to realise that the observer observes from their consciousness state and the doer does from their consciousness state.

These teachings are always available, always present, but it is you who has to choose to dive deep into them. There is the grace of the great spirit, the grace of the Mother and Father Divine and the grace of the teachers who are teaching. And then there is your own grace. As long as you are not willing to grace yourself with your own grace, the circle of grace remains incomplete. The grace of the spirit is available, yet we will continue to struggle as long as we do not openly declare that we are ready to learn. When we are ready to learn, to listen, there is a profound shift from that level of dejection, from being stuck in a victim state to willingness, a willingness to learn, a willingness to love oneself, a willingness to transcend. This declaration is a declaration of love and all love is directed toward self and so too is all hatred. So this surrendering and willingness to learn is a pivotal shift from the feelings of dejection and despondency; from waiting in the darkened room, door tightly shut, key inside the pocket, to taking out that key, opening the door and letting in the light. The key is always there, always in the pocket of the person who is locked inside the darkness. The only way this door can be opened is from the inside; the door to freedom cannot be opened from the outside. The door to supreme knowledge has to be opened from the inside. As long as you choose to keep that door locked, you can scream all you like but there is no keyhole on the outside. The keyhole of the door to your awareness is on the inside, you must choose to open that door. You must be willing to be your own friend, to be your ally. You must be ready to bless yourself. You must be ready to grace yourself. As long as you are not ready to grace yourself, you will stay locked in the prison of your own making.

That is the beauty of this relative field of reality. For each and every one of us is the infinite expressing in finite shape and form and free will is there within each individual. So within the play of the cosmic dream, everyone is given total authority to have their own experience without any interference. This is a very important teaching to realise, there is great power inherent within our own being. As long as we are unwilling to open the door which is locked from the inside, no light can enter. No matter how bright the source, no light can enter until we are willing to open the door. The brilliance cannot shine forth into our consciousness as long as we don't open up to it. Be aware, all your problems come from thought, for really this whole thing is humorous, life is fun, it is to enjoyed and celebrated, you cannot lose sight of truth. If you see the truth then the whole dream, no matter how terrifying it seems, is just a dream. Anyone who thinks there is a crisis going on is not established in unity. Bliss is one of the three qualities in being your pure Self, the nature of being in bliss irrespective of what is going on in the theatre of life. When you are in the same consciousness state that is creating the problem, you cannot solve the problem. The shared problem of humanity is the problem of conflict, of confusion, of a sense of crisis, of meaninglessness.

There is this obsession with overvaluing that objective reality and it is a dogmatic way of living. All objects ultimately exist within the subjective and it is that which gives value to any object. Even the value of what we call money is only relevant for the subject that is human. To a cow, a dog or a rabbit a million dollars has no value, no meaning whatsoever. Governments, passports, national identities, tax, none of these have any meaning to the birds. All things are relevant; they only have meaning within the subjective view of those who created them. This is a fundamental flaw within humanity that we are trying to solve problems only on the level of external solutions. What we do not realise is that problems are generated by the subject and as long as we are not addressing the subject, as long as we are trying to create solutions on the same level as the subject, we will keep generating problems. Endlessly. We call ourselves an advanced civilization but the problems do not seem to disappear. They are multiplying. For it is not the object that generates the problem, it is the subject. The knife is not a problem when you use it to peel an orange but only when you use it as a weapon. As long as the subject maintains the same consciousness state as the problem, the problem cannot be resolved. The consciousness state has to alter, then the problems dissolve. The consciousness has to rise up because only at an elevated state can one come down and solve the problem. When one is open to grow and evolve as an individual, open to the knowledge and the technology for the evolution of self, the self evolves and then life can evolve because as the self is, so life is. There is no life without the self. It is the self that lives the life. Life is nothing but an experience that the self is having. If the self does not alter their consciousness state and grow, life cannot alter and grow.

The nature of a transcendent being is ever blissful, all-knowing, timelessness; from bliss we have come, through bliss we are sustained and ultimately to bliss we shall return, for only bliss exists. We fool ourselves constantly, confusing our violent behaviour as philanthropy, as service. But as long as the self remains in darkness, all objective knowledge is useless. This is an important teaching for us to realise, that all our problems are only problems because they make sense to us. All our points of view come with these complex narratives we have attached to them. All problems exist with all their reasoning in the mind of the beholder. All opinions exist within the individual who holds those opinions with a certain level of justification. Even if that belief is as fantastical as the Earth being flat, that opinion does not come alone, unattached to complex reasoning. It comes attached to thought with a lot of reasoning.

A human life is an endeavour to escape three fundamental prisons: fear, ignorance and unhappiness. Every individual is looking to be happy. No one enjoys sorrow. It is important that each and every individual be honest with themselves and stop glorifying misery. Every individual is interested in the transcendence of suffering. We must accept that suffering exists, we must accept that misery exists, but we must also accept that we are deeply interested in the transcendence of them. Every individual is interested in discovering joy, bliss, happiness. Every individual is interested in transcending fear, ignorance and unhappiness. There is the unspoken fear within the ego because the ego is based on existential threat. It is threatened consistently by life, burdened by life. There is a crisis of meaning within the ego. It is afraid of time; it is in denial of its own mortality. It is afraid of the future, afraid of not being liked, afraid of not being worthy and it is trying to escape ignorance. That is why all individuals are interested in knowing; it is the nature of the being. Move in the direction of knowingness, move in the direction of unity, move in the direction of bliss, for this is the essential nature of Self. Self is moving in the direction of itself. The wise are established in their essential nature, they are not disturbed by the fundamental reality of life, of the relative reality. Remember, in time everything comes into existence and goes out of existence.

Compassion does not lead one to dejection, to a level of inertia, so we need to refine our intellect to be truly compassionate. The soul's nature is to be immortal; there was never a time that the soul was not and there never will be a time when soul is not. This is a direct invitation to us all to move in the direction of fearlessness, to transcend the conditioning, the attachments and not be afraid of death. For there is the spiritual death that one goes through when one goes into the transcendental nature of oneself, as one begins the journey inward, as one begins to withdraw the investments in one's ego self and let go one's narratives. The fear of loss is, of course, tied up with death but it is also the fear of losing oneself. If I am not this, if I let go of these stories, if I let go of these opinions, if I let go of these attachments, then who will I be? It is important to know this. There is total permission for every individual to live their life in the way they want. If one finds great meaning in complaining, then let it be so. If one finds great meaning in grief and sorrow, then that is fine too. These teachings are for those who are willing, who are now ready to go beyond the realm of struggle and suffering, beyond the realm of duality and who are interested in living a life of great bliss.

There is no such thing as death. There is only life and life is nothing but an experience the experiencer is having. And the experiencer experiences life from their consciousness state. The soul is the immortal presence; it is only the body that dies. One dies as one lives and one is reborn just as one has been living. So one can be stuck eternally in the ever-repeating known, playing the same story over and over again, repeating the ever-repeating known in the whirlpool. When we recognise our immortal nature, we see that all those around us are immortal too. Death comes to the body; the soul continues but it continues within the consciousness state of the body that has died. All life is an experience within the consciousness field of the experiencer. If the experiencer does not evolve, life cannot evolve. Life is an experience within the consciousness field; this is a profound thing to understand. As long as the consciousness field does not alter, life cannot alter. Different bodies, same experience. Different roles, same drama. Different theatres, same movie. Over and over again.

The moment we can expand our field of awareness, that which seems to be dominating our mind becomes tiny. When we develop mastery over our mind, we develop an equanimous mind. How does one develop equanimity? The nature of the lower mind is to constantly be busy with craving and aversion. It is either trying to avoid some experience or it is trying to chase some experience. This makes staying calm under pressure much harder. The wise one, meaning the one who is in a state of consciousness arrived at through the practice of yoga, is not tormented by duality. If you want to rise above duality, then you need to access that level of being. The techniques of meditation can elevate our status to the transcendental field where we are able to make contact with our pure being. Then we are able to exist in the relative field of reality, the 'real world' with its constant duality, in an equanimous manner. Without having access to the transcendental field, without having access to that level of pure being, it is not possible for the individual to be equanimous.

One cannot just convince oneself one is calm and emotionally stable if one is not; that is a suppression which will ultimately lead to a depression. Or an explosion. Equanimity is not just a way of thinking, of convincing yourself; it is borne out of a true experience. That is the technology of yoga. As we go deep within, then we are naturally able to have skill in our actions, skill in how we live our lives. Equanimity is one of the first qualities of the higher mind, a mind which is now becoming refined through the practice of yoga. If we are stuck in the lower mind, stuck in the cycle of craving, aversion, craving, aversion, always chasing and never satisfied, we are not equanimous. It is important for us to realise that the relative reality is the field of duality. What we are seeking through our yoga practice is a certain level of depth, a certain experience, and that level of experience is only possible when we go beyond duality. We cannot find stability within this reality for it is in a constant state of flux. Within every expression of it there is duality, polarities exist. So if the soul does not have access to the transcendental field, it remains stuck in duality.

Raise your status to that higher level. For the wise are able to ground themselves in their transcendental nature. They are not pulled by duality, not split by duality. To the yogi, the polarities do not seem as opposites; the yogi experiences them as expressions of one unified whole. The light and shadow are no longer opposites. The light and shadow are expressions of one living experience. The emotions of happiness and of sadness are no longer opposites, they are part of the living experience. But if the soul does not have access to the transcendent level of reality, then it remains caught up in all of this. Equanimity can only be accessed by diving deep into that level within our own being which is beyond duality, which is our pure Self. The soul which is not tormented by duality anymore begins to gain immortality. The wise one who reaches equanimity is able to perceive their own essential nature. If you are not able to perceive your own essential nature, all you perceive is time and time is death. Birth and death, birth and death, birth and death. This immortality is not some magic pill so you can 'live' forever or a computer program to transfer your consciousness into. This is the immortality of the soul. When the awareness is able to access its true nature, it begins to see who it really is. The wise one, now knowing their essential nature, starts to experience immortality. They are no longer disturbed by life, by the realm of duality. They exist in duality while simultaneously transcending it.

Through the practice, one is naturally accessing that transcendental level of consciousness, that pure ground of being, while refining and correcting the intellect. Then one naturally starts to gain fearlessness. For fear belongs to the domain of time; fearlessness belongs to the domain of timelessness. As long as the soul knows only time, there is always going to be a certain level of crisis, a certain level of fear within. The only way to access fearlessness is to access the timeless domain of being. So the immortality is the continuity of the existence of the soul. Death does not exist at that fundamental level. Death exists only on the relative level. One can only begin to gain this level of equanimity by accessing one's transcendental nature, by diving deep within one's own being. The fundamental nature of reality, that which is real, can never cease to be and that which is unreal can never come into being. This is a brilliant insight: that which is real can never cease to exist, that which is unreal never comes into existence.

Only infinity exists, finite does not exist. The finite only exists within the context of infinity. It is only the infinite that exists. So all shapes and forms that we see are all permutations and combinations of our own infinity, just as the wave cannot exist without the ocean. The wave is the expression of the ocean; the ocean expresses through the wave. If there is no ocean, there is no wave. The ocean within the context of the wave does not come in and out of existence; it is the wave within the context of the ocean that comes in and out of existence. The ocean remains, the wave rises and falls back; the wave does not have any existence independent of the ocean. You cannot see a wave without seeing the ocean. It's not possible. It is only the ocean, only infinity, that exists. So all shapes and forms that we see are ultimately expressions of that infinite consciousness. All that we see and perceive is ultimately an expression of our consciousness. Shapes and forms do not exist. It is only the formless that has reality and all forms are within the formless. The formless exists and the form comes in and out of existence; it has existence within a certain level of perception but at the fundamental level it is only the formless that exists. Shape and form rise up within space and time. All shapes and forms including this body are events within the infinite play of being. Just as the dreamer dreams the whole dream into existence, all the characters, the events and locations are all dreamed into existence by the dreamer for only the dreamer exists. Fundamentally, the dream has no reality. But of course, to the dreamer within the relative experience of the dream, the dream is real and naturally it is experienced as such. This is not a decision made on the part of the dreamer; it is the law of nature. Even though it is only *that* which exists, *this* is *that* so *this* should be treated as real. Those who deny the reality of *this* roam in darkness while those who deny the reality of *that* roam in darkness because *this* and *that* are ultimately an expression of the one living reality and the wise one exists at both levels, simultaneously. All shape and form come in and out of existence but the great Spirit does not come in and out of existence. All other experiences come in and out of experience but the Self exists and all experience comes within the consciousness field of the Self. This is such a brilliant teaching. Only that which does not come in or out of existence can be said to truly exist; the imperishable that is Spirit, pure consciousness, pure being, the great void, different names referring to that dimension of truth.

The soul is never born and it never dies for it is the unborn, everlasting. The body is born and the body dies but the nature of the soul is consciousness, pure awareness. Everything that we see and perceive becomes evident to the Self but the observer cannot be observed because on the subtlest level the nature of the observer, the nature of consciousness, is formless. All shapes and forms can be observed. The flower comes into existence within the field of awareness and goes out of existence within the field of awareness but the awareness existed before the flower came into existence, so the flower exists in relation to the awareness. And when the flower is gone, the awareness remains. The awareness is aware of the presence of the flower and is aware of the absence of the flower. For there to be any presence of the flower, there has to be the awareness of the absence of it. Just as when we sleep. When you awake from a deep sleep, you are aware that you were sleeping because there was an awareness of the absence of sensory stimulus. Then when you wake up the brain activity ignites, senses get excited, a certain neurological activity occurs. So there is the awareness of the sensory perception and the awareness of its absence. Awareness does not go in and out of existence, the nature of soul is awareness. All experiences come in and out of existence within that awareness. For you to know light, you have to know the absence of light. That is the realm of duality. Awareness is the constant; it is not born and does not die. The soul is never born and never dies. The nature of the soul is pure consciousness and we are the soul; we are blissful.

Only the body is born and only the body dies; waste no more time, evolve and grow. Refine your consciousness state for fundamentally, that is the only purpose of life. Without evolving, without refining your consciousness state, you will only experience crisis. The confusion will not end as long as the self does not transform. This life is our invitation to experience these teachings not just on the level of the mind, but on the level of being. This is a key point, it is important to refine and correct your intellect but then take it further and awaken to a deeper level of knowing for even when the body drops in death, the soul continues. How? It continues as the consciousness state and it expresses again. So one can be stuck within the ever-repeating known, playing the same character in the same story over and over and over again with no end to the problems or one can evolve. Truth is born out of experience not born out of thought; you cannot think yourself out of the loop. The teachings of yoga do not merely proclaim a belief structure but rather they give a direct experience of truth and the great opportunity to develop ourself in both directions, both levels of being, the relative as well as the transcendent. Grounded in that state of yoga, we are able to express elegantly and become clearer too.

Problems will come one after the other, for there is no end to the problems because they grow well in the fertile field of ignorance. As long as that field of ignorance is maintained, there is no end to the problems. Whether it is your relationship or your job or your government, whether it is the media or your friend or your dog, the problems will continue forever for the field of ignorance is where they flourish. So instead of staying stuck at that level, wipe out the field first, address the ignorance and clear it out. Otherwise, you can go on and on just digging up problems and trying to solve them. This is a very profound teaching and takes time to be understood, not just accepted but understood, because that which you understand you cannot forget. If you understand the teaching fully, you can never forget it.

Lesson 3

On Skill in Action

So if we are already that supreme Self, why can't we just remain as we are without doing anything, without confronting ourself? Why do we still have to act? It is an interesting dilemma, this contradiction. Many spiritual seekers experience exclusion from the mainstream; they find that being spiritual somehow means to become disengaged in the activities of life. Children are taught how to become a part of an already existing system. No child is educated to face a situation like this, the battlefield of the mind. So this is a beautiful insight into the dilemma that is faced by humanity. To say one believes in something is not to know it. There is a split where the knowledge can remain but it is not on the level of experience; the concept does not match the experience. But this is an integrated approach to growth not a reductionist one. When you come face to face with a teaching which is designed to lead you into a state of integration, designed to uplift your status, it is very natural for you to feel a certain level of confusion in the beginning because it is not a reductionist teaching. It is expansive. It is a holistic approach, a comprehensive knowledge.

If just the knowledge is enough, then why do we need to practise? We must clear up this misunderstanding. The way you are observing this teaching is specific to the consciousness state of your intention and although it seems like these are two different aspects, they are ultimately united; the path of knowledge and the path of action are not two different paths. No one can remain inactive, so how can there be a path which is action-less? To engage in knowledge, activity is required. The two fundamental aspects to the teaching are knowledge and action. The contemplative and the meditative. They seem different, but they are part of the whole. One might take on a certain aspect of the teaching but ultimately one has to find unity, one cannot attain freedom from action. This is the integrated state of being.

Just as in nature, when you observe a mountain, what you see is a profound state of stillness. Yet within that mountain is hidden an incredible level of dynamism. Stillness and dynamism coexist in every expression of nature. Even in a deep state of meditative awareness, when you are in that profound state of stillness, there is dynamism within it. Even within your body, when the body is still from the outside, a lot of activity continues within. You may appear to be doing nothing but you are doing everything. So this state of inaction is not the cessation of action, it is not inertia, but rather it is a dynamic stillness. By doing less you are achieving more. A tree is both dynamic and still. The lake is both dynamic and still. The sky is both dynamic and still. Dynamic and still simultaneously coexisting. In that deeper state, wisdom and action are inseparable, for to contemplate there is a certain level of activity required. To be able to take that knowledge from the conceptual to the experiential, action is required. The denial of action is a recipe for disaster. We are propelled to act. That is the nature of us as beings. We are existing within space-time, as we have expressed within space-time and we must use this dynamism to move in the direction of greater stillness. Then stillness and dynamism begin to coexist. When there is a consistent action directed towards evolution, then that action spills over into the relative field of reality and expresses as skill in action. And that is what changes the world.

If we do not align our action in the direction of knowledge, in the direction of evolution, we will move in the direction of regression. Time means change and in time you will act because the path of knowledge and the path of action are not separate. They coexist. Depending on the individual, some people might start with an asana practice or by being in the service of others, some might start with kirtan or with devotion. Some people might start by just listening to great knowledge, others by reading the scriptures. The starting points can be different but if the individual wants to progress, they need to unify because progression means a state of integration. One can be in a rush to reach a certain conclusion because reaching that conclusion gives one a false sense of security but as the awareness starts to get tired, the intellect starts to get tired. One feels a certain level of safety in reaching a conclusion because the state of not knowing is scary to the ego-mind. But an intellect which has been informed by the Divine does not get exhausted. Those who try to

On Skill in Action 51

control their senses artificially, by force, are denying their senses. Their minds still constantly wander and try to engage in the sensory realm. People who remain at that level of consciousness, who do not access the deeper state of consciousness, who are not using their inner energy to elevate their status, who are artificially suppressing their senses, are causing themselves harm because that suppression of desire leads to anger and frustration. It is an artificial cessation; the individual has not transcended or elevated their consciousness state. This kind of hypocritical nature causes suffering. We see it around the world, where people have taken a vow of certain sensory deprivation without the technology to elevate their energy and it has resulted in all kinds of complexities, all kinds of perverse behaviours. Sometimes they are expressed externally but a lot of the time it happens internally, creating all kinds of mental states. Using that energy, moving it in the direction of higher spiritual centres, in the direction of unity, instead of suppressing it, creates evolution. Those who use the energy are the ones who begin to discover the Self.

Remember, the five senses are not our enemy when we master them and align with them. As we draw up the energy, we are naturally refining those senses so therefore naturally lifting our desire. That is the teaching, the command to act is for yogic action, spiritual action, worthy action. What is worthy action? The action which is elevating the status of self. Don't just pay it lip service; embody the knowledge. To awaken to that deep level of knowing, you require a certain level of practice, actively engaging with the knowledge, actively engaging with the wisdom. This is an integrative practice, not just one particular technique; the spiritual action that honours the mind-body energy honours all the aspects of being. If you ignore any aspect of being there will be a lopsided development, so use your energy in the direction of elevation. We are being given the instruction to perform inward action and also external action, to engage in an act of service. But we must be careful here not to fall into the trap because if one is not refining one's own consciousness state when one is serving, then one can get into a saviour complex. A lot of people start with this idea of being in service to others, of saving, saving the world, but without the refinement, one is prone to misunderstanding the whole thing.

So, using that inner discipline, that inner fire to burn away the resistance, the inner resistance, that opposition to our own happiness that we have, leaves us in a state of inherent joy and joy gives rise to the state of desirelessness. Then the desire can come and go but the joy stays. Desire can arise and be fulfilled, desire can arise and not be fulfilled, but joy remains. This is not just talking about performing fire ceremonies to burn away the resistance because only doing the rituals on the external level, without the enlivening principles, without the meditation, is of no use. One can go to the temple and ring the bell as many times as one likes but this is just an external expression of devotion. To believe that devotion alone will somehow liberate you without putting in the work, that obviously is not going to happen. Rituals are a specific technology used to align ourselves with the aspects of our true nature but if one just stays on that level then one gains nothing. That is the trap. The external, ritualistic expression without the inner transformation means nothing. But as that internal awakening is going on, that will naturally pour out into the external values as well. As within, so without.

This is the movement from ego to awakening, from mundane to cosmic consciousness. This is a shift, where the Self is not just experienced in the sanctity of one's own silence but starts to be within the relative field of reality, experienced within life. Then there is no place where one does not see the light of consciousness expressing itself. The sacrifice one has to make in the beginning is the sacrifice of our lower tendencies, our grosser tendencies. We sacrifice them to the fire, feed the fire to keep it burning, cleansing us because to awaken to a certain level of greatness within, one has to make a certain level of self-sacrifice. You have to be ready to step up, you have to be ready to engage, ready to face yourself. Those who want to absorb everything without giving, to take and eat and engage in the pleasures of life without offering anything, without contributing anything, just take without giving, only suffer. You want to achieve a great life? Let me tell you, there is no such thing as a great life or a perfect life. There is no such thing as a great life; there are only great people. Great people have great lives and great people are not born. One of the greatest contributions that you can offer totality is your own elevated consciousness state. There is no such thing as a free life. The only free life is lived by a free individual. As you evolve, you free yourself. As you engage in right action, in evolutionary action, you start to live a life of service. You do not just do it for yourself, you do it for others. Then everyone starts to benefit from your progression. Everyone starts to benefit from your realisation. Everyone starts to benefit from your evolution and when you go deep into your own spiritual practice, into your meditation, into your silence, into your devotion, you're not just doing it in an isolated manner because it is uplifting the whole world. Through your practice the whole world starts to be lifted up. Human beings are looking for archetypes, so live an exemplary life. Rise up to your greatness for everyone around you is looking for an example. Be the example; be that which you seek.

As you begin to rise up, you will see what happens within your families, with your friends. As you begin to rise, lead from a place of compassion. As you begin to be that voice of sanity in the midst of chaos, you will naturally find that your influence will grow. Live in an exemplary manner, for we are all leaders; lead by example, don't always be pointing out the faults and problems of others. Become great, become an example, that is how you change the world. That is how you change societies. That is how you change cultures, by being the living example, being the Buddha in your family, in your society. Be your best, rise up and radiate. Any situation you face, be the sage in that situation. Align yourself with your greatness, feed the fire of greatness within you. For as the great do, so do others.

There is no duty for us to perform and yet we are active, the potential of unity is in all of us but we have to live the teaching, not just share it. Live your life as an example of constant service because that is uplifting. The

On Skill in Action 55

whole world is an activity within consciousness. The whole world is a play of the Divine. It is a pulsation of that great void, coming into existence spontaneously and being sustained by that pulsation of the formless. That is the Divine. Any moment if that pulsation ceases to be, nothing will exist. This body that you call yourself only exists to yourself. On the level of ego, you do not know how you exist. There is a mysterious force which gives you the experience of I am-ness. There is life but what is it that is maintaining that life? There is something greater than the isolated value of self, which is right now sustaining life. There is an activity at the fundamental level of being. Your very heartbeat, at this moment, is the activity. It is the Divine sustaining all of creation and also embedded within that creation. From the yogic perspective, the creator is not separate from the creation. The creator is within the creation, creative intelligence is within and without. Within nature there is a constant dynamism and that energy is constantly creating, maintaining and destroying. There is a vibration which allows the play to go on, for the breath to move, for the heart to beat. To deny the creative intelligence, to deny there is something which is greater than the isolated nervous system, is one of the greatest acts of arrogant ignorance. The effortless activity of the creative intelligence is like the wetness of the water, the warmth of the fire, the radiance of the sun. The radiance of the sun is not an activity of the sun, it is the nature of the sun. If we are not aligning this dynamism in the direction of progression, in the direction of love, in the direction of light, in the direction of unity, in the direction of harmony, in the direction of knowledge and wisdom, then we are paving the path for self-destruction. The unwise act from a place of ego, so their action naturally has a destructive value attached. The wise action has the value to uplift; it will have a life-enhancing quality to it. The result that is generated from that action in the relative field of reality enhances the experience of life. The action that is generated from unwise, ignorant behaviour only produces more suffering. It has immediate effect.

Do not confuse wisdom as just information. The wise one established in the Self, moving in the direction of their true Self, should not disturb the ignorant. Don't explain yourself to someone who is asleep. Let the one who is asleep, sleep. Don't scream and yell and force them to listen to you. Let them be. There will be a time when they will wake up but you must act, you must do your practice, you must be your best. Then those who are ready to wake up will see. For every individual has the right to live their life, to express their own consciousness state and act out of that consciousness. The lighthouse does not have to go chasing the ship. The ships who are not ready to come home will not come home; the ones who are ready will use the lighthouse as a guide. The wise do not need to disturb the ignorant. Just do your practice, improve yourself and you will always be victorious. No forcible conversions are recommended in the yogic tradition, just radiate and be the light that guides when it is required.

This is an invitation to each and every one of us, to be able to exist in the dimension of our humanity and our divinity simultaneously. In one's spiritual practice, as one dips into the ocean of cosmic bliss, drawing the energy up, stabilising the mind, smoothing away the grooves made by memories, then naturally the mind begins to become established in cosmic awareness, in cosmic consciousness, in the spirit. As you begin to acknowledge and experience that spirit within, then naturally all actions that arise in the relative field of reality become acts of service; all actions become actions of evolution. We do not have to let go of the fundamental nature of reality while engaging in the cosmic dimension but if the nature of Self, the nature of spirit, becomes totally overshadowed by relative activity, then how can one serve? By keeping your awareness on the Divine, not just your thoughts but your actions too, you develop that skill, that ability, to maintain a transcendent level of being. You are able to maintain the awareness of spirit, of your own cosmic nature, while simultaneously engaging in the relative field of reality and being part of this life.

The attitude which is essential here is the attitude of service, what can I offer? Then all our actions become actions of offering instead of actions of taking. Remember, the action of the wise is an act of offering. Actions from the ego-mind are only based on what one can take, what one can get. This action is naturally designed for failure because that is the law of nature. Whatever you offer comes back to you, so if you offer nothing that's what you'll get. This is an invaluable law. 'I' as an exclusive value of awareness will always be in conflict with the greater value. One has to take the 'I' in the direction of the cosmic Self. One has to take the mind in the direction of the cosmic Self. In the beginning there will be a certain level of effort because the path to effortlessness is through effort. One cannot reach the state of effortlessness without applying effort first. The action that arises from that consciousness state naturally reverberates, creates a vibrational field of that particular value, and that vibrational field naturally creates experiences. It draws energy to itself which reflects the same value back. Even the wisest ones among us, those established at greater levels of consciousness, still practise not from a place of no effort but from a place of natural innocence. That state of natural innocence is reached not by mere thought; it is reached through mindful action. One cannot just think oneself into that state because it is not a state of thought. Thought is on the peripheral level of consciousness; this is subtler than thought.

The wise will follow the teaching. The ignorant will constantly find fault, using their mind to work against themselves. This is foolish, arrogant behaviour, the arrogance of the ignorant. Those who are stuck in that arrogant ignorance are constantly engaged in fault-finding instead of practising. But this is a choice that they are making. We are all free to choose, no one is cursed or punished for their choices. But the choices we make do bear consequences. For that is the law of nature, what you sow, so shall you reap. No one can escape that. All individuals act out according to their tendencies, their imprints, their consciousness state, and that consciousness state is the result of the content of one's consciousness; it's what you've put in. But remember, the wisdom that you gain also becomes part of that content. Even when the body drops, that which you have accumulated on the level of your consciousness will continue and show up again in the soul. That is from where we get the idea of an old soul. So every individual is acting from their tendencies, from the content of their consciousness which has been accumulated. So one does not want to change just on the level of behaviour; one wants to clean away the imprints. For changing just the surface value will not take away the lower tendencies. Those tendencies will rise up at an opportune moment and find a different way. So use the energy to lift up your consciousness state but not to forcibly restrain it. Lift up through intelligence and address those tendencies. Don't just repress them, cleanse them.

Within the sensory potential, duality exists. All senses have preferences but don't take these sensory preferences too personally. Don't be swayed by the lower nature of the mind, don't get too attached to these preferences because as one grows and evolves those inner tendencies will change, then naturally what one likes and dislikes will change. In every sensory perception both craving and aversion are there, coexisting, likes and dislikes, but they are just expressions of one's tendencies. The preferences are predominantly arising from the conditioning, from the imprints within us all. What you have experienced creates those likes and dislikes; they are only on the level of the lower mind. So it is important that you don't get so attached to the sensory perceptions. You have to learn that you don't need to like or dislike everything. You don't have to agree or disagree with everything. For if you are busy liking and disliking, then you are not growing. As you evolve, then you develop self-mastery and the senses are behaving as per you instead of you behaving as per your senses. One's senses are so beautiful, so amazing if they are used properly. Learn to harness your senses.

This is the brilliance. It is not only about the whole field of creation but also about our sensory perceptions; the whole scope of knowledge can be discovered here. A lot of the resistance to the is-ness of is-ness is generated through the senses which are anchored within those tendencies that are caused by our conditioning. We have certain tendencies inherent within us and those tendencies get projected through our senses onto the objective reality and then everything, depending on what has been projected onto it, reflects that same value back to us. And that shapes our world. One has to realise that and stop taking things personally. One should not remain too focused on the level of sensory perception, trying to always get the optimal experience just for the senses. That is where a lot of our activity is wasted. The unwise waste a lot of their time in just creating a life which can meet the preferences of their sensory perception. The foolish, instead of paying attention to what is being asked of them, instead of doing that to the best of their ability, have too much interest in other people's business. This is a recipe for misery. A lot of the people are miserable because they think that the person next to them is happier than they are; the person on social media has more likes than they do, more friends, more followers. Instead of focusing on others, focus on what is being asked of you in the moment. Fulfil the need of the hour from a place of integrity. Be exemplary. In time it will be natural for you to fulfil the need of the hour with spontaneous right action, natural for you to follow the voice of your intuition. Resistance will be there in the beginning but this is just part of the process. One should not judge oneself if one finds this resistance, this confusion, arising within. That is to be expected. Just focus on yourself, on your practice, be exemplary in your life and stop poking around in other people's lives. This is one of the big diseases of humanity, to judge and criticize what somebody else is doing. The ego is a control freak. A true leader delegates authority because as one delegates authority, one has to step aside and let others do their best. And we all need to learn to do our best in whatever we are engaged in. Focus on that. Be of service, offer that into the heart of the Divine because all activity in the relative field of reality should be an extension of cosmic consciousness.

So why do individuals act in a regressive manner? If it is our fundamental nature, the nature of our soul, to be in bliss consciousness, why do we act in a violent, regressive, ignorant manner? What makes us act out in such a way? It's a good point. This is all part of our conditioning, part of the play of nature. This kind of activity arises from a certain consciousness state and, as we know, our consciousness state is a result of the content of our consciousness. There are three aspects of that conditioning: conditioning that happens as we grow up, what we were exposed to when we were young through our family, our school, our friends and so on, which all imprints on the level of our psyche. Then there is what is going on on the collective level of the planet during our life. And then there is the personal evolution of our soul through the different incarnations. No one wants to suffer; nobody gets up in the morning and says let me have the worst day possible. Nobody has those intentions. Yet mysteriously, we find that there are those who seem to act in that way, as if propelled by some kind of invisible force. Because as long as those latent tendencies, that conditioning and those imprints we have collected, are not being cleared out, then the behaviour will continue, the suffering will continue. Just as a fire is covered by smoke or a mirror by dust, so too is knowledge covered by desire. Those seed memories will give rise to desire and that desire will give rise to a certain kind of action. That action will confirm and solidify that memory, burying it even deeper into our unconscious. The construction of desire happens at the level of the unconscious and if that unconscious, that information base, is not being shifted then the desire keeps being regressive. The individual seems to have no control over the self but those who have a slight level of awareness will be able to see that their desire is moving them in the incorrect direction. Those who do not have any awareness do not see how their desire is propelling them at an escalating rate towards destruction. We must gather up our energy and move in the direction of that greater Self for that is who we truly are. That is the highest action one can take; that is the action we must take. Because only when the energy starts to move, when the awareness starts to move in the direction of Self, can one master the mind. As we begin to master our mind, then the desire which is arising from those imprints can start to be refined.

Lesson 4

On Knowledge Leading to Bliss

These teachings have a timeless quality. They have a timeless relevancy to their wisdom and are not dated chronologically because irrespective of whatever space-time location one is in, every individual is interested in finding greater joy, greater knowledge, greater fulfilment. From the yogic perspective, there has always been the idea of eternity but within space-time there is a cycle. Things come into manifestation, a teaching comes into manifestation, and in the beginning stages it is very pure, very clear but as time moves on it starts to become diluted. This is natural because the teacher teaches from their state of consciousness and the listener listens from their state of consciousness. There is a gap between the teacher and the listener on the level of consciousness. Now, if you remove that by 10,000, 20,000, 100,000 then there is going to be a certain level of dilution in the teachings and their essence can get lost. So even though the nature of this wisdom being shared is eternal, in time it goes through a process. It rises up in time, it gets stabilised in time and then in time it gets perverted and lost. In any movement there is the innovation, the early adopters, the early majority and the late majority; any movement has these four stages. We speak of a timeless tradition and a timebound tradition. A timebound tradition often needs to be broken. The timeless tradition has to be honoured. This is about sharing wisdom from the source, the eternal flow of knowledge. But within any tradition, this dilution, this perversion of the teachings, can happen. To gain this supreme knowledge one has to first ask, one has to be genuinely interested. For if we have love and receptivity, we can transcend anything.

You may ask, if we have been in existence time and again, over and over, why don't we have any recollection of it? We have forgotten all of it but within the memory remains because that is the nature of cosmic, god consciousness. All memory is constructed in consciousness. Remember a certain slice of time in your life, maybe when you were fourteen. If you think of yourself at fourteen years old, it is like thinking of a different person, yet you still remember it because the awareness of yourself at fourteen is still there. The awareness is maintained but there has been a change on the surface value, you no longer look like yourself at fourteen. In the cosmic mind, the cosmic consciousness, that slice of time is always in the now.

If you look at the context of light in time, for example, then no matter what speed you are traveling at if you measure the speed of light, it will always be the same. So your movement does not have any effect on the speed of light; from the point of view of light it is always at all places. Just like space, in the context of space there is no location because all locations are within space. From that cosmic state, there is memory of all, all that needs to be known is known. In the cosmic consciousness, all is available in the now. The body is born and dies but the cosmic nature is ultimately timeless; the nature of supreme being is subtler than time, pure consciousness is subtler than time. Time arises within awareness, within consciousness, but the nature of the Absolute is subtler than time. Time devours everything but the Self devours time. Like the dreamer who dreams the whole dream into existence and becomes all the parts and the scene, everything that is within that dream is both the dream and dreamer of the dream. Their consciousness is the dream: the characters in the dream, the setting in the dream, the emotions that are going on within the dream, the whole experience of the dream are all from the mind of the dreamer. The dreamer is not just a character within the dream, the dreamer is everything that exists within the dream, the whole dream. Decades can pass within the dream, only a few seconds can seem like eons. There is nothing that exists within the dream which is outside the scope of the dreamer. So this is a metaphor for the manifest reality.

Great knowledge will always lead to great bliss. The wisdom when practised will always prevail because nature favours evolution and the desire of the supreme being is evolution, is progression. The dreamer of the dream wants to enjoy the dream. No one wants to have a nightmare. If the dreamer starts to have a nightmare, they want to correct it, they want to wake up. Evolution is always available; the stream of wisdom, that supreme knowledge, is always available. Even in a deep level of crisis, the moment we become willing, we are able to discover the wisdom in these teachings; they are always available whenever we are ready. And as we take on the teaching, the ignorance gets wiped out; whenever the ignorance starts to become stronger, the course can be corrected, the ignorance can be wiped out, the conditioning destroyed. As we start to awaken, the conditioning starts to be undone. The attachments that are stuck within start to be cleared out. The fog that clouds our third eye starts to get cleared. Our infinite potential which has been suppressed starts to rise up. That is the birth of cosmic consciousness. Unity consciousness. We cannot take this teaching in isolation; we have to see it all as a whole. We know already, we first have to be a willing student to receive these teachings. The knowledge is available whether we receive it or not but we have to do the practice. We have to rise up to that knowledge and we have to discover cosmic consciousness.

So the knowledge is always accessible, our own higher Self is always available, and as you start to apply yourself to these teachings, what happens is the destruction of ignorance. We know now there is no saviour coming; there are teachers, guides, enlightened beings to offer instruction if the student is willing to learn. The wisdom will always be available. Evolution is always possible; ultimately the light prevails. This is the play of life, the play of the Divine Mother, the play of consciousness. There is always progressive change happening and the divine play always goes on. If the only thing that is, is the Absolute and the Absolute is the only thing that exists, then where does evil come from? It is all part of the great creation. This is not about believing. This is for those who are willing to learn and rise within the intimacy of their heart, within their own being. The instruction is very clearly to practise now, not to wait, not to believe in anything, but to practise.

When the wisdom starts to rise in the individual, all the ignorance starts to be wiped out within. So of course, it then gets wiped out collectively too. For each and every individual represents a universe unto themselves. Because a universe is an experience, you are an expression the universe is having. You are the eyes and the ears and the body of the universe. You are the doorway. You are the window through which the universe experiences itself. We know this, we have met people, been touched by these beings who are established in a very specific consciousness. The quality, the flow of their energy, the radiance of their being, is very unique. And this radiance is accessible to each and every one of us. That is a brilliant message here. Many have realised cosmic consciousness through that deep devotion, deep reverence, by taking the energy to the higher spiritual centres, by taking the mind to transcendental ground, by clearing out the intellect, by transcending fear, transcending attachment, transcending anger; that is how to realise living enlightenment. This is about living enlightenment. Living bliss. Living a life in bliss consciousness, in love, in light. Such a beautiful teaching. For all beings are seeking that but they seek in their own ways. What is the law of nature? Whatever one seeks, cosmic consciousness will respond to.

How beautiful is that? What you seek, you shall find. All beings are following the path. What is clear to the wise can, for those who are not yet awakening to wisdom, be a little bit confusing but that is intentional. Confusion on that level is intentional. The confusion is the invitation to reach a deeper level of understanding, to not become complacent, to not think, "Oh, I got it all" because the field is a self-responsive system. We live in a universe which we can see and it responds, it is a self-referral system. What we feed into the field, the field feeds back into us. What you feed into the system, the system feeds back into you. As I say, whatever you seek, you shall find. Whatever point of view you hold onto tightly enough, you will prove yourself right. If you hold onto any thought deeply enough, about yourself or others, then that thought will be fulfilled. You will have ample opportunity to validate that thought; the universe will validate it for you because whatever you seek, you find.

When consciousness shows up on the level of the human form, when that supreme being expresses at the level of human, then there is a certain level of freedom to think, to contemplate, to ask questions. So at the human level, the choice becomes available to us to choose what we seek and whatever that is nature will support it. We will find confirmation and that seeking is not just on the level of thought. The seeking is on the level of being. What level of energy you are maintaining, whatever level of consciousness you are vibrating at consistently, nature will organise things around that and will deliver that. Every individual is looking for something greater: greater joy, greater stability, greater peace, greater comfort, greater

On Knowledge Leading to Bliss

safety. And the only answer is wisdom, to be on the path of self-realisation. It is only the Self that will answer the questions because it is a self-validating system. The universe is consciousness and you are consciousness. There is only consciousness. So whatever you are interested in, whatever you are consistently putting your attention to and aligning yourself with, nature will deliver that to you. Whether you consistently engage in self-evolving action or self-destructive action, ultimately the fruit of that action starts to be born. Because you are informing the universe and the universe is informing you.

One must be aware of the traps, of getting lost in the ritual, of taking the word literally. If you don't practise totally, if you just read the words, you won't get it. Be an integrated being. Engage with it, act on it, be ready when the need is upon you. There will be different needs at different times and one has to engage with them. At a certain time, there may be one dominant expression and at another time another dominant expression. When you need to stand up and be the warrior, in that moment you have to be the warrior. When you need to gain knowledge, move in the direction of the supreme wisdom, refine yourself, then move in the direction of your cosmic Self. There are moments where you have to serve, be in humble service which wipes out the ego-mind and at times you have to inspire people, but you should not be teaching all the time. All these are activities that we have to be ready to engage in because if we do not, then we remain a fixed person, an incomplete individual. They are within each and every individual; these activities are what we have to be able to fulfil when the need is upon us. We have to be creative. We have to add to society by creating something of value which enhances the quality of life, engage in worthy exchange for it is the law of nature.

If you are very much aligned with your higher Self, then the actions that you are engaging in in the relative field of reality do not create imprints; they no longer create conditioning anymore, they no longer create bondage. Otherwise, every action which is not arising from that consciousness state, that deep dive within the transcendental nature, will create bondage because every relationship creates complexities, every interaction can create a potential conflict. So those who start to become established in their true nature will no longer be bound by their actions because a state of fulfilment is being reached at the transcendental level. The action is no longer manipulative, the action starts to become more and more natural. At that level spontaneous right action becomes more and more available and it elevates the status. The one who has accessed the fire of wisdom within themselves becomes free from their past; all the bondage of karma from their past gets wiped out. But of course, that requires a certain level of practice, that is very clear. It requires a certain sequence, a certain process to be gone through. It is important to realise that it is the present that is the cause of the past, not the past which is the cause of the present. To those in the state of ignorance, the past is the cause of the present. They are stuck in this chain of cause and effect and so create the same patterns over and over and over again but the fire of wisdom burns away the seeds of karma, meaning freedom from the past. When we engage in those subtler practices, we find we start to become free;

On Knowledge Leading to Bliss **71**

the mind starts to become free and is no longer bound by the repetitive patterns of our thoughts. The memory which is stuck within the body starts to move out.

It is very important to remember not to hold other people's pasts against them and not to hold your own against yourself. Everyone has to take responsibility for the actions that they have committed but when one really commits to the path of evolution, one can undo the past and change the course of the future. You can start to change the influence of the past upon yourself but as long as you are not free from conditioning, you cannot discover the Divine. So one has to look at one's conditioning and become free of it by bringing up the wisdom. One has to really begin to identify oneself at the deepest level of the soul, to realise oneself at that level, then one starts to become free from the bondage and clear it away. The three dimensions of conditioning are: conditioning on the level of your present incarnation, conditioning on the level of the earth-time and conditioning on the level of your continuous reincarnation, so it is never too late for anyone to start doing the work. When one can learn to see in that way, then we are able to have compassion and we are able to forgive. Some are then able to clean certain aspects of their psyche, some lessons need a deeper cleaning and as long as that cause is not removed, the effect will keep being generated. So if the same consciousness state is maintained, that effect will keep affecting you no matter where you go. You have to be locatable at a different dimension of reality, a different dimension of consciousness. If you maintain the same level of consciousness, the karma will keep affecting you. You will keep getting caught in that same whirlpool; you will find the same story repeating in your life over and over again. As long as the individual is not ready to radically grow at the deepest level and transform on that level of being, then the karma repeats. With the practice of meditation, the mind starts to become free from certain repetitive patterns of thinking and to develop insights. As we develop our insight and we are able to have a deeper level of alertness and awareness, we are able to resist the temptation to engage in those repetitive karmic patterns of behaviour and we slowly self-correct. This creative intelligence will then slowly express itself further and wider.

So what is action and what is inaction? It's a good question and the one who sees action in inaction and inaction in action is a yogi. They are able to come to that place within themselves where the action contains inaction and the inaction contains action; these two seemingly opposing qualities are merged. Of course, this is on different levels. Firstly, the level of the spiritual practice. To the untrained eye, when someone is in a state of deep meditation, it appears that there is nothing going on. But to the practitioner, as they dive deep into that state of inner practice, they start to experience that state where the practice just happens on its own. In that state of deep meditation, there is a certain level of dynamism and that dynamism, that activity which is arising, is also on the level of the body. These are fundamental changes that are occurring on the physical level. Changes start to occur on the energetic level too, on the level of your consciousness. For in that profound state of deep, transcendent stillness, there is dynamism; in that deep state of meditation these experiences start to arise spontaneously. That action leads you to inaction and within that inaction, that state of transcendent stillness, dynamism is maintained. All practitioners who have gone to a deeper level of practice understand this principle. On the surface it seems confusing, inaction within action, but for anyone who goes deep into the practice, they realise the merging of this inner state of profound stillness where the body is not really engaging in any external activity yet has a very different kind of action. The result of the practice only the practitioner can see; inaction and its effects remain hidden from other people around them. The effect is an intimate experience arising within the being. That is where the action and inaction merge, where one begins to experience that merging of stillness and dynamism. The calmer you are, the more present you become and the more starts to happen. The stillness in this very moment, the stillness that you have access to, actually gives you a deeper access to the field of dynamism, to knowledge. This knowledge which is arising, this wisdom that is flowing in this moment, sits deeper in you if it is in the presence of stillness.

For those with the untrained mind, there is a constant struggle between action and inaction. They cannot come to rest within themselves; they need to escape themselves. Something pulls at them, they are not enough because when one comes into that space of stillness without proper knowledge, the self wants to run from the Self. So there is a constant struggle between stillness and action, between action and inaction. But in the deep state of that inner practice where there is a certain level of stillness, dynamism is occurring; there is a unity in that. When you begin to understand this principle, then it begins to show up in your relative field of activity as well. The wise one, when acting in the relative field of reality, is able to maintain that inner level of presence. That inner level of stillness itself becomes a surrendered action. The idea of doer-ship starts to fall away. That is the state of you channelling the work that needs to happen, you becoming a channel of creative intelligence because in stillness you will find more happens; the less you do, the more shall happen. This is the principle of yoga; doing less is not on the level of effort, it is a consciousness state. The experience totally takes over the effort so instead of you doing something, it starts to just happen. When the doer and the doing merge, a state of flow starts to arise. That is the flow of genius moving in you; that experience is the unity of action and inaction.

When we merge with that activity, whatever activity we are engaged in becomes meditative. That quality of unity starts to create a flow of activity, the state of flow which is a flow of brilliance that starts to happen through us. On the intellectual level, all action is in collaboration with the extended Self. It is not just the mind-body which can generate brilliance, the brilliance must be generated in collaboration with the extended Self. The isolated self cannot generate brilliance out of stillness. The isolated self remains stressed. The soul identified with the ego-mind is the isolated self, so when it goes into stillness it struggles. It does not know how to be with itself. It wants to escape from itself. When it goes into the domain of activity, it gets stressed out and exhausted. So the domain of activity creates the experience of struggle. This is the dilemma of the egoic mind. The soul identified with the ego-mind struggles in the domain of activity. It struggles in the domain of stillness. It struggles within itself. It wants only to escape itself. All activity then becomes an escape from oneself and it becomes very difficult to be with oneself. So the one who finds action in inaction and inaction in action has found the clue into the supreme integrated way of life. Even as we are engaged in an activity, once we are able to access a certain level of stillness in our activity, genius flows. The stressed, isolated self, cannot express genius. Any individual who has expressed any level of genius knows that one gets into a certain state of flow. Whether it is writing, playing music, gardening, any level of activity, the more you feel there is no action in it, the greater the genius will be. Let's say you observe a pianist, a master pianist, you will see that their mastery is reflected in an effortless manner. The pianist's fingers are gliding over the keys and it looks easy, they are in the flow, there is no gap. That is the expression of mastery in any domain of activity. The seemingly complex activity is expressed with innocent simplicity and if you ask the pianist, they don't even know how they're doing it. Any individual who has experienced that flow of creative genius says, "I was in the flow." There is that moment where the effort disappears, the struggle to get it done disappears, and it starts to flow. As that creativity is flowing through you, you start to get excited, you do not know how you are doing it. You are doing a lot more but there is a stillness within it. That is the inaction in action. The flow of stillness.

The nature of that activity itself is extremely nourishing. When the individual is in the state of flow, they are nourished by it. The activity does not leave you exhausted; the state of flow, of genius, is the spontaneous, correct action that starts to happen. The practices are designed to render us capable of this ability, to be able to drop into that flow state more and more. While engaging in that, there is a state of surrender, this is the surrendered action. Without that state of love, without that state of union with the greater Self, with the field of the Divine, this skill cannot be available in all domains. It can show up in a particular isolated skill set like playing the piano but for this unity of action and inaction, inaction and action to occur, there has to be the birth of the integrated being. The relationship of the self with the greater Self has to be one of love, of trust, of surrender; the universe outside has to be experienced as an ally, not as an enemy. That surrendered state is a state of supreme courage and wisdom and gives birth to this ability to be doing your best while being surrendered. You realise that your actions and the result of those actions don't belong to the isolated ego-mind structure; there is a greater process at work for any result to occur. You are engaged in activity, but there is no sense of ownership over it. Any wise one understands that. The ego-mind is forever stuck in the state of control because it is scared. It wants to control and the more it tries to control, the more it loses. For the fundamental law of the relative field of reality is that there is nothing under our control. The more you try to control the field of infinite variables, the more you will lose. It is a recipe for defeat and we are interested in a victorious life. From a state of surrender, we can find victory. To the mind this seems to be paradoxical but to the wise this is a very natural and intelligent way. Surrender means victory, control means defeat.

The idea that life is happening to you is just a thought. In the awakened state you know that life is happening for you. Cosmic consciousness is life happening through you. This state of life happening through you, the action happening through you, is the state of inaction in action and action in inaction. Dynamic stillness. Stillness in dynamism and dynamism in stillness. For ultimately, what flows through you, what creates through you, is that cosmic, creative intelligence and as long as the egoic mind holds tight and resists that flow of intelligence, it is threatened by that greater Self. Then there is stress, physical stress and mental stress. Stress leads to all kinds of disorders within the body and the mind, life becomes a struggle; that is the experience of the existential burden. To be still is unbearable. To be active is unbearable. We see human beings finding it very difficult to be still within themselves. To be with oneself becomes a very troublesome invitation for a lot of people. People crave activity, to be constantly busy, then they feel justified to act in an unkind, unaware manner. "I'm too busy" is the favourite mantra, "I have a lot on my plate." This is the way of the fool, not the wise one. The wise one can be engaged in extreme levels of activity, fulfilling the need of the hour while remaining surrendered, allowing the action to happen through them. This is not a particular mood you can decide on; this is a state you have to cultivate within yourself. You have to be able to consistently experience this state where you are in the flow within yourself, where the action takes over and you enter that transcendental state where the creative intelligence takes over and the egoic mind fades. Then you can bring that out into the relative field of reality and experience stillness in your action.

You will accomplish so much more by being still, by absorbing instead of doing: then victory is guaranteed. In this stillness, absorbing the supreme knowledge, the whole world fades away as you enter into a state of flow because a lot is being accomplished in that stillness. That is the impact. When this state starts to be cultivated, the wise one can accomplish a lot without making any noise about it. We must train ourself to access that state, that surrendered action; to be present and still while being active. That activity can have the supremely fragrant quality of inaction in action and action in inaction. When we begin to bring this principle out, this flow of genius into our environment, then what we create is in alignment with the law of nature. When we create from the stressed consciousness state, what we create is not in alignment with natural law and so creates all kinds of stressful situations for the creator as well as those who are engaging or consuming that which has been created. But the creation which arises from alignment, where there is a unity being experienced which flows from that, nourishes not only the creator but also the one who is enjoying or receiving that which is being created. Both are nourished and liberated and the effect on the environment of that activity is of an uplifting value. Just as in nature, the universe creates from a still centre. In the relative field of reality, there is constant activity of creativity occurring from this profound stillness.

The one who is able to embody this quality of action in inaction, inaction in action, naturally starts to live a life of purpose, moving away from being stuck in that ever-repeating whirlpool because within one's consciousness the fire of wisdom has been lit. When the fire of wisdom is lit, ignorance just burns away; this is a transcendent state of understanding. When the light of awareness is switched on, it is not a progression from that state of ignorance; it is the transcendence of that state. One can remain in that state of ignorance for as long as one likes and one will not learn anything good, because one's whole premise is based in ignorance. As long as the light of awareness is not switched on, there is no wisdom. But for the one who has wisdom, the light of that wisdom burns away ignorance immediately. If you walk into a dark room and switch on the light, you see everything clearly, all of it, immediately. You don't wait for it to slowly become visible; the whole room is clearly visible as soon as you hit the switch. Switch on the light of wisdom and you realise the absurdity of the whole situation, the human condition, immediately too. Only the one who is experiencing enlightenment on a certain level can know the others who are experiencing it for they do not proclaim themselves enlightened. It is only someone in whom that quality is being born who can see that quality in others.

As you begin to discover that inner ocean of bliss and the transcendental level of being, it's not a matter of belief. You are able to know. That inner state of supreme unity rises up, swells up and fills your heart with a state of fulfilment; the intellect starts to find fulfilment by diving into that ever-increasing knowledge. This state of fulfilment leads you to a state of self-referral bliss. That becomes the natural state and one can draw the senses and the mind within, dive deep into that ocean of bliss and rise up in fulfilment. Then you are no longer seeking anything, no longer trying to manipulate the world because the world is now supremely magnificent. If there is ever going to be bliss, it has to be here and now. You are not in the waiting room, not waiting for something to show up or someone to show up because you are naturally in the state of appreciation, the state of awe of the miracle that is the here and now. One of the main reasons why the mind misses the miracle is because it is consistent; the Divine is always here so the mind misses it. But it is consistently here, always, in your every breath, in your heartbeat, in everything that surrounds you. It does not come or go; it is always here. And because it is always here, the untrained mind misses it because it's constantly busy looking for something which is not here. This is the state of the foolish, they don't experience the miracle that is here and now. Nothing is missing, this is the state of fulfilment. This state of fulfilment does not mean that desires will not arise. The state of fulfilment means that the fulfilment remains even when the desire arises. Desire arises and the desire is fulfilled; desire arises and the desire is not fulfilled but fulfilment remains. This is the state of integrated being, engaging in the field of the Divine, in the here and now, and remaining in that state, remaining in that state of unity. There is no sense of doer-ship. This sense of doer-ship, this sense of accomplishment, creates a very strange personality. But the one who is impacting many lives in a positive manner remains innocent. That is the quality, remaining innocent while doing nothing. That is self-referral bliss.

The human mind is designed to move in the direction of more. That is what leads to progression. But contentment is not birthed out of what you have or don't have. Contentment is born out of the experience of your essential nature, by elevating yourself. When that state of elevation starts to arise, this experience of inner bliss will arise, this capacity where you can be engaged in the relative reality in the here and now. Then this profound peace starts to take over. That is what contentment is. That state of unity that starts to emerge where the Divine is experienced, where the relationship to reality is of love in the here and now. One is freed from jealousy, from a state of hatred of oneself and of others for jealousy is a double-edged sword, cutting someone else as it is also cutting you. For one to experience the state of jealousy, one has to be hating one's life. One rises above jealousy not by the suppression of jealousy but by cultivating that state where one begins to thrive in one's life. When you are living a life of joy, a life of unity, then there is no jealousy for jealousy is born out of discontentment. You're just not happy with yourself, at ease with yourself, with who you are and what you're experiencing. One transcends this state of jealousy because one is thriving.

So to transcend this jealousy, one has to begin to thrive. And as one transcends this jealousy, then naturally one's influence grows. Greater magnetism arises because one looks at people and situations as allies whereas the egoic mind looks at people and situations as competitors, as opposition. This shift to seeing people and situations as allies creates a great state of magnetism. People are drawn to those people. There is nothing that is not consciousness, it is not just isolated within the human. Consciousness is all-pervading. The knower is consciousness, the practitioner is consciousness, the practice is consciousness. The experience that arises from the practice is consciousness. The knower, the known, the process of knowing and that which emerges are all consciousness, are all the Divine. Knowing this is the fundamental truth of life, of living fearlessly.

Using the symbology of fire as an action in the service for evolution, a certain level of sacrifice is required, meaning to let go of that which is not serving you. You are able to engage and feed that which supports progression and unity, while you're also ready to let go of that which is a resistance to that unity. If you want to grow, there are two actions involved. In the beginning stages you have to intentionally engage with those actions, with modes of activity, modes of thinking which are progressive and then you have to consciously let go of the resistance. You have to sacrifice those narcissistic tendencies which show up as resistance. You have to consciously let go of that, that's the sacrifice. You have to feed your attention to that part which wants to grow while simultaneously sacrificing that part of you which shows up as resistance. And one supports the other. The letting go of these tendencies, these narratives, these influences within you, supports the progressive behaviour. One has to be ready to sacrifice aspects of oneself which draw one in the direction of misery.

When you are offering wisdom to yourself, engaging consciously with wisdom, absorbing wisdom, you have to simultaneously let go of the ignorance. You have to be ready to let go of your own prejudices, belief structures, a certain worldview born out of your conditioning or you will never allow the light of wisdom to shine through. Through these practices, the cleansing happens. One has to engage sincerely in the evolutionary action without doubt. Doubt is the enemy of realisation, chronic doubt. It's one of the tools to keep one stuck in the same place, in the state of hesitation. It's one of the narcissistic tendencies of the egoic mind. This is not blind faith; it is knowing that there is knowingness, a knowledge field that you do not know yet but you are very interested in finding out about. For enlightenment is not a passive state, it is dynamic. In the state of chronic doubt, one does not move, there is no accomplishment. If one remains in doubt, one is inert and there is no end to that; it is mental chaos. The state of inner doubt is a state of weakness. Nothing can ever be good enough, nothing can ever be right. So it is unwise for us to engage in that mode of thinking. Anchor yourself in trust and use that energy to move in a progressive direction, doing action in the service of knowledge. True knowledge. As you engage in that, it's like keeping the curtain open. When you keep the curtain open, the sun rises and the light shines in but you must open the curtain first. The sun will rise in time but if the curtain is closed, the light is not able to come in and in time the sun sets again. So stay open to knowledge and know that time brings it all. In time the seed turns into the tree. Everything happens in its time, nothing before its time. Always now. Never then. Be open and let the light of knowledge in. You have to transcend the state of doubt. You can't talk yourself out of doubt, for doubt is nothing but a way of thinking. And the more you talk within it, the more you dig yourself into a hole. So transcend that state and act from a place of trust.

This world is to be enjoyed and to be celebrated. The cleansing is to be enjoyed and that which emerges is to be enjoyed. The mind revels in the experience of bliss that arises in you. For those who cannot find joy in this life, what hope is there for them finding joy beyond it? This idea that if you suffer now, struggle now, be miserable now, then you will be happy when you die is incorrect thinking. Life is not a punishment. And death is not some kind of a rocket ship bound to somewhere else. There is no heaven or hell except the heaven or hell of your own making. Heaven and hell are here because there is nowhere else to go. Celebrate your existence here and now. The command of this teaching is to come out of the waiting room because the being who does sacrifice the narcissistic tendencies which show up as resistance, all that doubt, does find joy. If you cannot find joy here, where does it live? It is born out of this cleansing process that you have to go through within yourself, the refinement of your own intellect, of your own understanding. If you cannot come to that place here and now and rejoice in this magnificent miracle that is consistently happening, then when? I assure you, you will not find it anywhere else.

On Knowledge Leading to Bliss

If one is not moving in the direction of knowingness, of awareness, of great wisdom, then one remains within the domain of what one knows. Knowledge is the driver of action. You act within the domain of your own knowledge and the way you think is generated by your worldview. Your worldview shapes your behaviour and your worldview is shaped by the knowledge you have access to. What one thinks is possible and what one thinks is not possible are all within the context of the worldview that one holds. It is only the light of wisdom that burns away the ignorance, the incorrect knowledge. Understand that knowledge, the power that is within wisdom, and discover the truth. Seek out the seers of truth, join the golden chain of Master to student, student to Master. Every Master is a student. Every student has the potential to be a Master. It is an endless chain going all the way to the Absolute. Know the power of wisdom and serve the seers of truth; ask them to teach you. Don't just believe in something, go and learn, go and serve, ask questions, for without worthy inquiry, there cannot be any delivery of wisdom. Without the curtain being opened, the light cannot come in. Don't believe, learn; develop that thirst for knowledge, that passionate longing for evolution. Find the source and learn because knowledge has to be learned. Seeing is not believing. Seeing is seeing.

There is always hope for everyone, irrespective of what they have done in the past. No matter what transgressions they have committed against others or themselves, they must forgive. Dive deep into the fire of wisdom because the possibility of transformation is available to each and every one of us. Acknowledge where you have transgressed and then move, progress; no matter how far you have transgressed, you will still be able to transcend. This is a clue. There is no reason to get attached to shame and guilt. That is all in your mind and will keep you locked down in the deep dungeons of depression. Irrespective of what you have done, irrespective of what has happened, acknowledge it and then offer it into the fire of wisdom. Apply yourself here and now instead of getting stuck in the dungeons of doubt, shame and guilt; use the sword of wisdom. The sword of wisdom will shatter into pieces the shackles of ignorance. Ignorance confuses the soul into thinking that the shackles are an essential requirement for safety, that the ignorant belief systems, the falsified identity, are necessary requirements to be safe. Instead, be set free, not safe but free. There is no one judging you, for love is available equally to all. Judgement only exists in the absence of love. This universe is a universe full of love, it is a forgiving universe. Forgive yourself and sail on the raft of wisdom across the sea of bliss.

Lesson 5
On Letting Go

Should one renounce the world or act? These two aspects are important for us to understand and it is our eagerness to understand, not our weakness, that can often lead to confusion. This is important for individuals who are sincerely on the path to know. Individuals who are sincere in awakening to a deeper level of knowingness with a genuine inquiry have a certain discernment. That is part of the learning process, a certain level of questioning, a certain level of contemplation. Mistakes are part of learning. Any culture, any system of learning, which does not allow mistakes becomes regressive. That is why the wise ones always give total permission to everyone to commit mistakes. As long as one is willing to learn, mistakes are very welcome. When the individual becomes afraid to commit mistakes, then they cease to learn. When one is committed to the process of learning, mistakes are a natural occurrence within that process. The questioning in a dilemma actually presents a window of opportunity for learning. If there is no questioning on the inside at all, then the person is shut down and walking around with arrogant ignorance; there is no learning and progression ceases.

To act or not act, leave the world or engage with it? It is a natural tendency of the human mind to be reductionist, there is a gap in the understanding but for the wise, the path of renunciation and the path of engagement are not two different paths. On the surface they can look very different but they both feed each other. One cannot reach wisdom without action and action without wisdom. Action informs wisdom. Wisdom informs action. They go hand in hand. It is only the ignorant who think these are two different distinctions. They are distinct only on the surface level but as you go deeper, if you want to really progress, then there has to be a state of integration; you have to find unity. If the call of the spirit is to step away from the world, then that's how the spirit speaks. But if the spirit in your heart says to stay and be a part of it, then that is wonderful too. One is not better than the other. They are different only on the surface level. Whether one is living in the cave or in the city, if one wants to progress, then one has to reach a state of integration; if one wants to evolve, one has to reach a state of integration.

Knowledge is supported by activity and the action supports the birth of knowledge. When the higher states of consciousness start to express within the relative field of reality, one starts to discover the sacred, one starts to discover freedom while remaining in the world, part of the world. One is in the world, but not of it. That's the true renunciation, not just renunciation at the surface level. The true renunciation is the elevation of consciousness. It does not mean that you are turning away from the world to live a solitary life of denial; it means while remaining in the world, you are not of it. You have reached that state within yourself where you are no longer identified with the lower self, with the lower mind. And to reach that state, action is required. Practice is required. Evolution within and then one has to bring that out into the world of reality. Play in the Leela of life that is this world, while remaining established in the transcendent, cosmic world; realise the dream-like quality of this nature of reality, the impermanence of all that is seen and perceived. So from the yogic perspective, to realise your own god nature, you don't have to withdraw from the world because one can be here and there simultaneously. One is aware of the impermanent nature of all reality while being established in that pure ground of being. For an integrated being, the state of letting go, of supreme detachment, that state of non-identification, is reached through the practice. And through the wisdom, the practice is deepened and one starts to wake up to one's own essential nature. As you wake up to your own essential nature, you are naturally able to rise above the world while also engaging in it. That is the nature of the wise: being in the world, but not of it; playing in the joy of this life but simultaneously being available to the transcendental ground of being.

Without mastering the mind, the senses, the energy and awakening the heart, how can one hear the voice of the higher Self? One has to master the mind, that is at the base of the yogic practices; through meditation, kriya, wisdom, through refining of the intellect, one slowly starts to master the mind. But the mastering of the mind is an integrated process. One has to educate the mind properly for it is hungry for knowledge and needs to be fed supreme wisdom, needs to be exposed to greater awareness. What is the law? Whatever you expose your awareness to most consistently, you will start to become that. Whatever you expose your mind to most consistently, your mind will start to take on that value. Through meditation, you start to dive deep and as you start to enliven the awareness at that level of being, the mind starts to naturally, spontaneously become filled with peace and greater joy. Naturally the senses become refined as the energy starts to move in alignment with a high value of life. Otherwise, the sensory experience remains depleting. Through the practices, one awakens and is able to master the mind, refine the senses, open the heart and find liberation. The heart is the seat of cosmic consciousness; the heart is the seat of love.

Through mastering the mind, gaining that state of deep silence within not by forcing it, but by using the appropriate technology of meditation, of drawing the mind into silence, refining the senses, moving the energy up and awakening the heart, cosmic consciousness is born. Each and every individual knows that when you experience deep love, you do not experience it in your left knee or your right big toe, you experience it in your heart. It's a visceral experience. When you experience compassion, when you are moved deeply, you can feel it in your heart, the seat of divine love. But one cannot just bring the heart online by blind faith. The mind is a great servant, but a terrible master. That is why the tradition of meditation is a base practice, to create that inner silence, refine the senses and awaken the heart. It has to be an integrated approach. As the heart starts to be awakened within the individual, the being starts to realise the Self and wake up to the play of life. The veil starts to become thinner. You can see beyond the obvious and you can start to identify that one consciousness moving within all. It is not a belief but a visceral experience. When the truth becomes a visceral experience, then it is fundamentally liberating. And as you start to become aware of your true nature, start to experience a certain level of unity, then the actions in the relative field of reality cease to have dominance over you. Just like the lotus leaf which remains untouched by the water, the drops sit on the surface of the leaf but do not get absorbed, so your actions become more innocent, purer, and you remain untouched by the play of life; life becomes a dance and is no longer a battle. Transcendental wisdom is now arising; life is being lived on two planes simultaneously. That is the life of renunciation and action, detached action.

We all have authority over ourselves and each individual acts out from their own consciousness state. On the level of our individuality, participation is always required so if the being is identified with the ego, then they act out and fulfil their own destiny from that place and bear the fruit of their own actions. But the Divine, the transcendental, supports any level of consciousness irrespective of what belief system one has. Life goes on and any activity one chooses to engage in is through the prism of one's own consciousness state. So when we speak about the Divine working through us, we are speaking about a certain level of alignment that is a conscious alignment. It is an active surrender. The individual is not propelled by an invisible force which is deciding what they should or should not do. The presence of the Divine is always here, it is an unconditional love; there are no conditions, one is just free to be. At the deepest level one is that, one's true Self, and at the relative level, one experiences oneself not as that, yet the creative system at play continues to work itself out.

There is no god sitting somewhere in his office with a bunch of accountants adding up what you did or didn't do. This world is a self-organising system and within that system evolution is supported, progressive change is supported. For ultimately within the relative field of reality, there is a certain level of trajectory which is designed for greater and greater evolution, greater and greater unity, and at the core of that is bliss. So when bliss arises in the soul, that bliss finds greater confirmation because that bliss is in greater alignment with the essential nature of being. And as love is the essential nature of being, it thrives. But if one chooses to live from a place of anger and blame, resisting the light of truth, the universe still goes on. Flowers still blossom. Birds still sing. Saturn still moves. The greater cosmos is untouched by the human drama, but one's own experience is determined by one's consciousness state. The stars keep shining brilliantly while the individual can be in total denial of the magnificence of such beauty. The beauty doesn't complain though, the beauty remains beautiful. It maintains itself even if the individual is passionately in denial of it, for in the relative field of reality, the supreme being has delegated this authority. Every individual within the human incarnation has the right to be right.

As that wisdom grows, that light of knowledge which starts to shine in the consciousness of the individual, a lot of the attachments and the ignorance start to naturally fall away. The problems you had at the age of sixteen seemed very important but as you got older you realised how absurd they were. So it is that as the light of truth starts to shine, you start to see the absurdity of this whole thing. You begin to realise the meaninglessness of it all. And as you begin to discover the true wisdom, that which was falsely created through structures of thought, through perverted knowledge, just falls away. If that is not happening, then there is still work to be done. But if you can see how your behaviour is changing, then it is a natural sign of truly growing up within yourself. When the light of wisdom is illuminating your issues, the narratives and belief systems, the ideas and opinions that you held so dear, all those constructs start to crumble. Then you can have a giggle about it, you're no longer afraid to laugh at yourself. Because if you are not able to laugh at yourself and laugh at yourself hard, then there is still need for growth. But as you grow and evolve, you can laugh at yourself and you can forgive yourself. For just as you have to forgive everyone else, you have to forgive yourself too.

So the intellect is being established and refined through the light of wisdom. Once you start moving in the direction of unity consciousness and you start to elevate your awareness, liberation begins. Once you have seen the light of truth, you cannot un-see it.

Then as the awareness begins to rise in the direction of unity consciousness, it starts to dominate one's perception.

Unity does not mean the absence of diversity for in the relative field of reality, diversity is the law. The higher stages of consciousness from ego, awake, cosmic, god, all these stages of consciousness are degrees of unity and as one starts to establish and refine one's own energy, one begins to gain access to greater and greater unity. At first, as this experience gradually starts to rise through the consistent practice, refining your intellect, exposing your awareness to greater knowledge, that unity is experienced primarily on the level of one's own individual existence. But whether it is in the elephant, the priest or the tree, there is that one unified field of being, that one unified field of energy which dominates the entire intergalactic space. On that level of being, where energy and consciousness are intermingling, there is no boundary.

All boundaries are structures, fluid structures within the boundless. The boundless is arising and being perceived through a certain level of perception where boundaries emerge. As the consciousness starts to rise, one is able to witness that one being, that one consciousness, that one supreme, transcendental being expressing in all relative fields of reality. Then what starts to naturally happen is harmony starts to dominate, love starts to dominate, and within the relative experience of life, one can live in greater and greater states of consciousness. That supreme consciousness is expressing itself and rising up as the tree, as a mountain, as a human, with different scales of organisation, different levels of complexities, but the fundamental base reality is indivisible. This is known on the level of the intellect and it is known on the level of feeling and then it is known on the level of experience.

On all levels of knowing, this experience starts to rise and dominate instead of diversity and boundaries dominating. For as long as boundaries are dominating, there is threat. But as the consciousness state starts to evolve and these isolated values begin to merge, love starts to dominate. It is known on the level of the intellect; it is known on the level of feeling and it is known on the level of deep experience. And then it can be lived. To be very clear, boundaries are honoured. One still meets the elephant as the elephant, one does not become incapable of cognizing boundaries. One includes them and yet transcends them; the activities within the human play of life remain but are transcended. They are no longer the dominating value within the field of one's own consciousness. This is the life of liberation, a life of living enlightenment.

The steady intellect is born out of a deeper cognition, a deeper experience of being. It is born out of the elevation of energy. It is born out of correction of one's assumptions. An intellect which does not have an understanding of higher dimensions of wisdom and is fundamentally just based on accumulated information does not remain steady. For the steadiness of the intellect is arrived at through the steadiness of being. The intellect remains shaky when the experience is not grounded in being; when the energy is steady within oneself then the intellect becomes steady. Then one can live without doubt and that chronic hesitation is replaced by awe and wonder. When the soul is in the state of deep identification with the lower self, there is a chronic doubt, this existential threat. The individual is never fully here because there is always a level of hesitation. This chronic doubt has to be transcended. As long as there is still this state of chronic doubt, the brilliance within cannot be birthed and one will always be held back. For one to give one's best, there has to be an absence of doubt or one will always hold back from pouring all of oneself into what is being asked of one. Action without hesitation, that is action in unity. So for greatness to arise, there has to be that absolute state of commitment in whichever direction one moves. Then naturally, one starts to become free from the pulls of duality and one is able to meet life with an open heart and a sense of wonder instead of a sense of hesitation. The ego-identified being is constantly meeting life with a sense of hesitation, as if life were against them.

Those deep states of equanimity are arrived at through the practice of yoga, of meditation. This is an important thing to realise. The fundamental purpose of the yogic practices is not just for stress management. Yes, they help in the transcendence of stress and in optimizing health on all levels but that is not their fundamental purpose. The fundamental purpose is the elevation of the status of self in the direction of unity. Every day, when one dives deep into that field of silence within, the flow of attention is reversed away from the external and toward that profound stillness. This gives rise to the value of truth within the mind where dynamism and stillness merge. In that awareness, the mind rises up and gains in value. This is all achieved through the natural technique of meditation which is why it is the base practice in yoga.

So those who start to move in the direction of unity naturally find that their actions start to be uplifting for all beings. This is an important thing to realise; goodness cannot be born out of an unrefined self, an unexamined self. If the self remains unexamined, the activity of the self can never be consistently uplifting, can never be consistently progressive. If the only knowledge one has access to is based on one's conditioning, then one's ideas of good or right are created through that conditioning and are not in alignment with the fundamental needs of the hour. It is a totally biased understanding. The relative field of life is incredibly diverse and it requires an untainted mind. It requires an intellect which has access to the cosmic field. It requires a stable awareness. If the self remains at the dense levels of understanding, then the self's relationship to life is based on threat and stress and conflict. If that is the experience of the self, then the actions will always have that value. So even when one thinks one is acting intelligently, one is not.

If we are interested in being of service, if we are interested in making a positive impact, an elevating impact for the benefit of all, we can only do so when there is a movement in the direction of unity. Then there is an elegance being born within the sanctity of our own experience. If that is not the case, then all actions in that field will have a certain strain of manipulation. If one is not refining one's intellect, not expanding one's wisdom, not examining one's prejudices and one's fundamental assumptions about life, then actions that are born out of those unexamined assumptions from that fabricated sense of self, of a self born out of an accumulation of different imprints of conditioning, are not the result of a consistent flow of intelligence. A lot of perverse actions arise and the interesting thing about it is that the perpetrator remains oblivious to it. The harmonious influence of the Self in the relative field of reality can only be born out of the experience of harmony within one's own being. That is the dynamic state of wisdom. Only from the wise one who is experiencing these deeper states of Self, who is elevating their consciousness, can actions start to be uplifting. Just by the way they innocently interact with someone from that loving, kind heart, genuinely, authentically, can ripples of progressive change in the field of reality be felt. Remember, true impact cannot be measured. The one who is elevating and awakening their own inner potential, radiating it out, naturally expressing it in service, starts to have an elevating influence. All their actions start to be innocently elevating. So when you are evolving, when you are refining, when you are living a rich, contemplative life, when you are diving deep, you have to realise that you are not just doing it for yourself, you are doing it for the whole. As you rise up, again and again, the influence ripples out into the field to promote the wellbeing of all sentient beings. That is the law of nature.

Drawing the senses inward, focusing on the third eye, stabilising the breath, lifting one's energy, naturally creates a consistent flow, elevates, stabilises the mind and refines the intellect. These are the techniques, different aspects of the integrated approach. By focusing at the third eye and drawing the energy inward, one starts to gain victory over the fluctuations, starts to discover liberation. The soul is not just a driver within the body; it is expressing as the body. The body is ultimately an expression of you and so when you work with the body, with your energy, your mind, you start to evolve. Your experience starts to change and that is the value of these teachings. The practice of integration and living in an integrated state creates an integrated value of unity, of equanimity, of love.

Working with our energy as we draw it up along the spine, we open up the super highway. As we go deep into that practice, senses are drawn inward and attention flows slowly and effortlessly in the direction of the third eye. In the beginning for some individuals, a certain level of effort is required; that state of effortlessness is reached only through effort. Even when we use a mantra for our meditation, we might find a slight resistance, a restlessness, but slowly, through consistent practice, one starts to transcend that. In time, consistency in any activity leads to the experience of effortlessness. Consistency is the key on the level of any practice. When the senses are drawn inward, instead of the attention being scattered in the relative field of reality, running from one object to another, one thought to another, focus is on the energy at the centre of the eyebrows, at the third eye. With the intention to liberate oneself, one discovers that that liberation is one's own essential nature. The gaining of liberation, that state of supreme freedom, one's own essential nature, has to be discovered and brought to life and then lived. It is available to all, within one's own being. When one experiences it, then one can live it. When one experiences the light of the Divine within one's own Self, then one sees it all around because that is all that exists. Remember, that does not mean that reality fades away and just disappears, absolutely not. The relative reality stays, but it does not dominate your experience anymore. That is an important distinction to understand.

People may ask, "If I get to that state, will I be able to still relate?" That question becomes irrelevant when you access that state because you will know how to relate. It's like saying, once I learn to ride a motorcycle, how will I be able to walk? You will walk when it is relevant and you will ride a motorcycle when it is relevant. But when you know how to ride a motorcycle, walking is not the dominant way to get from A to B anymore. Through these practices, drawing up the energy and focusing at the third eye, one can hit the cosmic freeway and allow the flow of perennial wisdom that refines and liberates the intellect. And the beauty of this wisdom is that it is not just met on the level of the intellect. When you dive deep into this, it is also experienced on the level of feeling and when you stay with it and you combine it with meditation, then it is born at the level of soul too. Remember this is a dynamic state, it is not static. It is not something you achieve and that's it. It is dynamic, consistently evolving, but the instruction is not forced, that stream of intuition is not forced. You can totally deny your intuition. You can totally deny the voice of your inner being. But when the student is ready, then living a life in love is available. Other choices are always available too and are all valid. It is an important thing to realise; the Divine is always available. Whether one is always available to the Divine is the question. What is cosmic consciousness? It is the individual becoming available to the cosmos and the cosmos kind of taking over the individuality, cosmic intelligence acquiring an individuality.

It is very easy to stay at the level of the ego-mind, the level of the senses, the level of the noise, remain just within the made-up human universe and to really miss the play of life, miss the whole beauty of it. There's a lot more beyond the made-up human universe. To truly enjoy life, one needs to know the nectar that is born out of the practices, the nectar that is born out of unity. As one starts to create a certain culture of self, the result is bliss, the infinite rejoicing through its finite expression as the finite realises its own infinity, its own infinite nature. This movement of the finite value moving in the direction of infinity gives rise to supreme bliss, bliss born out of cognition, out of unity and experienced at the subtler level. Then it rises and swells up from within us; this is knowing the Self. That joy that is born out of the realisation of our innate nature is a joy which reverberates in the entire intergalactic universe. The influence of that activity is far greater than the influence of the activity which is just on the surface level. The activity of ignorance, the activity of destructive tendencies of the human psyche, is fundamentally on the surface level but the influence of the activity which arises from that deeper level of consciousness has a far greater influence.

There is a lot of chaos in the relative field of reality, human beings acting out from their grosser tendencies, but we find that love keeps prevailing because there are beings who are active at that deeper level and, even if fewer in number, they have more influence. As the soul gains that level of cosmic value within itself, as these greater states of unity consciousness are lived, the influence of that innocent activity is far greater, far stronger. When you act from love, then you act genuinely and kindly and that one kind gesture travels far and wide. The true impact, which elevates and liberates, cannot be measured.

Lesson 6
On Inner Unity

In the integrated state where love and detachment coexist, the path of renunciation and the path of action, the path of knowledge and the path of activity, are one and the same. Only an integrated approach can lead to the state of yoga. Only the one who has reached that deep union within oneself, while simultaneously radiating that flow of supreme consciousness into the relative field of reality, fulfilling the need of the hour while remaining undisturbed, unattached to the world, is truly integrated. This is not to be confused with just the external display of a certain identity. This is a state of internal unity. The state of an integrated being remains detached while infinitely loving, remains still yet simultaneously active, knowing everything and simultaneously nothing. That is the state of integrated being.

But in the beginning, effort is required. Once one is in the flow, effortlessness is required. In the beginning stages of one's awakening, there is a certain level of effort which is required because there can be a lot of resistance one has to face within oneself. But once one has gone through the initial stages of one's development, then the teachings, the practice, naturally start to lead one. There has to be that surrendered ease; you're not trying to get anywhere so your action naturally has a sense of effortlessness, a sense of ease, a sense of patience, a sense of presence. But for those who are not yet on the path, a sense of urgency should be there. For those who have arrived on the path, they need to relax within it. There is a merging that happens that gives rise to a meditative experience; action and actionless become one but the actionless state is not a state of inertia. You're not in a vacuum. It is the state of creative stillness.

Your own personal practice is important, being in your own aloneness. One has to lift oneself through one's own effort. If one is not willing to put one's own effort in the direction of elevating oneself, then even the creative intelligence remains helpless. This is an important key. The only opposition that exists is one's own self as experienced within one's mind, as experienced within one's own behaviour. Oneself is one's own friend or one's own enemy. One has to ask oneself, are you your own friend or your own enemy? When this friendliness towards oneself arises, then there is self-compassion, but also self-responsibility. Self-compassion without self-responsibility is incomplete and self-responsibility without self-compassion is incomplete. So self-compassion and self-responsibility are the two values that begin to flow within you when you take on the attitude of being your own ally, being your own friend, instead of being your own enemy. The one who has not transcended the identification with the lower self, the egoic self in the state of delusional identification with structure of thought, remains committed to acting antagonistically against oneself. One consistently acts against oneself, creates situations, experiences, self-destructive ripples, states of feeling and thinking which are all against one's own essential nature. For if the self remains in the clutches of this false identification, then there cannot be self-love. The ego-mind remains in this dual state of self-hatred and self-righteousness and that is not the state of self-love. This is a very important thing to realise.

It is natural for people to encounter this voice within because of a lack of proper understanding. The self-critique is the voice of the ego-mind constantly judging, hating, feeling they are not enough. Then one reacts to this voice and projects it, turns it the other way around where it starts to judge, criticize, isolate, reduce others and takes on the position of righteousness. We have all experienced this dual aspect of our own ego-mind, where we have felt less than everybody else and then we feel everybody else is wrong and we start to judge others because if the Self is not known, how can there be self-love? As long as the individual, the being, remains identified with the lower self, it remains a tormentor of itself. This consistently persistent illusion, where the burden of responsibility for your experience lies on someone else's shoulders somewhere else, must be transcended.

The power that generates your experience is not somewhere else, it's in you. You are the cause of your experience; you are not the effect. This shift in understanding from being the effect to the cause is the fundamental shift that declares maturity. As long as the soul is identified fully with its own lower self, with the illusion of self, it acts not in its own favour. So one remains the biggest problem in one's own life; oneself is the common denominator in all the problems in one's life. The lower self is the supreme generator of complexities, the supreme generator of problems, for oneself. This is a brilliant insight. Be a friend to yourself or be your own worst enemy, the greatest act of friendliness toward oneself is to know oneself. Transcend one's identification with the ego-mind, the false self, for that is the beginning of awakening. One's primary commitment should be to oneself. This is not narcissism or self-centeredness. This is about the realisation of one's own Self.

Through the power of meditation, through the power of practice, one is refining and diving deep into that transcendent absolute ground of being, gaining that supreme knowledge of Self for once the light of knowledge is lit, it lights both the inside and the outside. As one gains that supreme knowledge of Self, one starts to have access to the non-local knowledge which flows into the relative field of reality. That play of the Divine that is life has a knowledge field. The knowledge within is rising and that knowledge flows in specific channels. The access to that transcendental field of supreme knowledge then flows within those specific areas, a specific flow within the realm of cause and effect. It is the domain of spiritual science because there is spiritual science and the relative science and one becomes comfortable in both domains. That is the integrated being. Spiritually elegant, transcendent, wise but also very much able to engage here in the world, very clear and decisive in their activity. For knowingness flows in both directions, worldly knowledge and spiritual knowledge creating an elegant environment. Harmony will start to dominate within your scope of influence but only if you are interested in a life of integrated living, a life of illumination. Other options are equally valid, there is no one judgement. This is important to realise. There is no pressure to be one thing or another. There is total freedom.

One must learn to take time in one's aloneness, to dive deep and to know oneself or else one will only know oneself through others. We need to take this deep journey within and meet ourself or else we are only known externally, through our job, our relationships, the different roles we play. The only way to truly know oneself is to dive within the depth of one's own aloneness. That is where the Divine lives. The Divine is situated there within us all, it is just at a different level of perception, a subtler level of awareness. This aloneness we experience leads to unity. Drawing the energy in awakens our higher spiritual centre. Focus on the third eye as you engage in your meditation consistently and start to make intimate acquaintance with that baseline being. As one takes the seat of meditation, it is important to get the body in a particular state. Then one goes deep into meditation spontaneously. Sit tall as the spine has to be tall so the energy can move freely along it. As the awareness transcends, it brings up a state of elegance, of self-respect within oneself. That is the highway of energy. Now draw the senses inward, allow the mind to go into that deep, inner silence then let the body surrender. But when you start, always start with that elegant position, sitting tall. Through the consistency of practice, you will naturally progress. Consistency is the key. There is no magic wand; it's all about consistency.

The path of yoga is one of balance, activity and rest, the consistent, middle path. This is not a fanatic practice; it is all balanced. Only the one who is balanced in their activity and rest will progress. When the meditativeness starts to appear within us, we become like the flame of a candle which exists within a windless room, where the candle maintains a certain level of consistent flame. As that meditative state starts to arise within, the mind is no longer fluctuating, is no longer swayed. This state naturally becomes available to us in the relative field of life, this level of staying power, this level of ability to focus, to be present with what is instead of being constantly distracted. This epidemic of distraction, of scattered attention, is part of our modern condition. Remember, your attention is the supreme currency of life. You spend your life through your attention. What you are giving attention to, you are giving your life to. Whatever you give attention to becomes part of your life. So your attention should be like the flame of that candle in the windless room, steady and constant.

It is important to take care of this supreme currency, to be aware of where your attention is going. Be aware of how you spend your attention. Be mindful. Be alert. Remember the law, what you give attention to will grow. So whatever you want more of in your life, you must give it attention. Now for you to *give* attention, you must first have it. You cannot give something you do not have. You must ask yourself, "Do I have my own attention?" Do your thoughts have your attention? Does the media have your attention? Does the drama of your relationships have your attention? Who has your attention? For one must claim one's own attention. You must honour your attention on the level of thought and choose carefully what you give your attention to because, as I've said, it will start to grow. It will start to become a dominant part of your life. If the quality of what is drawing your attention is elevating, then it is a beautiful thing. But if that which is drawing your attention is depleting, then it is not recommended. The untrained mind is often fascinated by pain, by negativity; it is unfortunately the nature of the untrained attention. The untrained attention is fascinated by the drama of life and is drawn to the negative aspects, keen to latch on to the one bad thing in a sea of good, the one bad review, the one bad word. Mastery of your attention is found through meditation, through kriya. And you must realise that without training the attention, it will flow in the direction of negativity, of distraction, and this sucks out all one's energy. So it is important to learn to master one's attention.

Through the practice, one starts to stabilise and to see more clearly. Then as the disturbances start to subside, the soul is able to glimpse its own cosmic nature. As the energy starts to become integrated, as the soul starts to experience this inner universe, it starts to experience super sensuous joy, to move in a powerful way. As this inner, orgasmic experience starts to arise, one starts to experience the bliss within oneself and this bliss that starts to arise is of a supreme value. It nourishes the soul and naturally makes one free from craving; one naturally begins to taste that inner, orgasmic bliss and then the lower cravings start to disappear.

Established in this state of bliss, one has the courage to face the greatest of life's challenges because in this great journey in the relative field, change is inevitable. And within change, the experience of pain is inevitable. Pain is the gift of love. Pain is only there because there is the possibility of experience, so this bliss has infinite room for pain. When this inner bliss is not there, then we are afraid of pain. We are afraid of change. We are resistant to it. This resistance to pain generates sorrow and misery. The embracing of pain leads one to a deeper experience of compassion, a deeper experience of appreciation, a deeper experience of gratefulness. Pain is the gift of love. It is the price we pay for living a full life. But if this bliss is not there, then one does not have the guts to face this ever-changing field of reality which holds the experience of pain within it. Instead, one wants to escape it.

Lesson 7
On Realising the Self

The question, who is the creator, is a very natural one. The creator of an object is embedded within your awareness of that object. When you observe a watch, there is an understanding in your consciousness that there is obviously a watchmaker. It's a rational understanding, not a belief. You don't have a belief that there is a watchmaker. You are absolutely certain that there is a watchmaker because there is an organised system there, a certain mechanism which consistently performs the function of the watch. It is the same with the manufacturer of a glass or a table. The moment you see the glass, the glassmaker and the glass are already within your own awareness. The moment you see a table, you know it was made by someone; it is naturally embedded in your understanding. So you know it was the watchmaker who made the watch, you don't believe it might be. There is a certain level of organisation and that organisation has a certain function. A glass is an organised system. A table is an organised system. The watch is an organised system and that organised system performs a certain function. For there to be a watch, there has to be a watchmaker and there also have to be the essential ingredients which are used to bring forth the watch.

So there is the intelligent cause and the material cause, two fundamental causes for the creation of anything. You are already aware that without the intelligence there could not have been a watch, but when you see the flower, then what do you see? What do you see when you observe the mountain? What do you see when you observe the sun? Or the moon? Or the twinkling stars? What do you see when you see the bird singing? What do you see when you see yourself in the mirror? Somehow, when we observe the flower or the mountain or the bird, we think it has arisen out of something which is inherently unintelligent. The watch has an intelligent creator and so too does the flower. Any organised system requires two causes, intelligent and material. Everything that you see and perceive requires both. So we have established that anything we observe naturally must have a creator. There is an intelligence behind the watch. There is an intelligence behind the table. There is an intelligence behind the flower and anyone wise will seek out that creator. There are four kinds of seekers who seek the creator: those who are miserable and want to be saved, those who are desirous, who want something in return, those who are inquisitive and curious, and the fourth kind, the wise, those who realise the Divine within themselves, those who know and are not just seeking but realising.

So you can easily understand there is an individual who made the watch. You look at it and you know there is an individual who made it, but when you are dealing

On Realising the Self

with the intergalactic universe which is limitless, then the dilemma of the creator becomes very difficult. The nature of the manifest reality is that it is limitless, so you are dealing with a certain objective reality within which the objects are limited. But the reality itself is limitless. You need the intelligence and you need the material. Now when we are talking about the origin, the fundamental cause, that fundamental cause has to have both values within it. If it has to be created from something, then that something has to already exist. So who created that something? Everything has to have both values; they have to be inherent within the cause. For the creator ultimately has to have both values. The fundamental cause has to have intelligence and material within itself. Just like the dreamer who dreams the whole material reality into existence within the context of the dream. The material cause and the conscious cause are the dreamer; the intelligence and the material both are present. Anything that exists, exists through that because that contains everything. When you come to a point where there is nothing, that nothing has to have everything. The potential of everything has to be in that nothing. That is what the Buddha called the field of emptiness, the great void. That great void is not void of potential. We call it the void, we call it emptiness only because when the mind makes contact with it, with that transcendental field, it turns silent.

The Divine, cosmic consciousness, is the conscious cause and the material cause. It is consciousness itself which is modifying and showing up as matter. It is consciousness itself which is organising matter. Energy is intelligence, intelligence is energy. They are inseparable. So when we are dealing with that infinite relative field of reality, then the cause within its own self has to be infinite and that cause has to be formless but simultaneously all forms because all forms are within the form-maker. It is that pure consciousness that is everywhere, in everything. Infinite, formless, yet expressing in form for all forms are forms of the formless. All elements are modifications of consciousness, the earth, the air, the water, the fire, the ether, that sacred brilliance is embedded in every expression we see and perceive. Any object, any structure we find is impermanent. They are all events unfolding at different rates. The inherent intelligence which maintains the flower as the flower or the mountain as the mountain is natural to it. That divine consciousness is the fluidity of water, the radiance of light, the warmth of the fire and the fragrance of the flower.

So the fundamental cause on that level has to be infinite in its ability and that infinite ability cannot be located in some isolated space. It is embedded within the material reality, for the material of all that is manifest is actually immaterial. What you call matter is actually non-matter. That which does exist on the level of matter is a very limited part of any structure; the fundamental value of that structure is actually immaterial. It is inherent within the nature of that supreme Divine, for they are all modifications of that pure field of brilliance. It is the elements and the experiencer of the elements. For there to be matter, there has to be the experiencer of matter; for there to be the heat of the fire, there has to be an experiencer of that heat. The experience and the experiencer are inseparable. So it is that supreme intelligence, the Divine, that is the fundamental cause of all that exists and that cause is not isolated; that cause is embedded within the material reality. The field itself is the field of divine intelligence. That is the birth of the universe. The birth of the universe is from the womb of emptiness.

Since the material cause and conscious cause are embedded within all, then the Divine is located in all beings; the creator is within all beings and all beings are within the creator. So you cannot go looking for the Divine. For you to look for something it has to be separate from you. The creator is the created and it is naturally evident in all expressions and values. To know this, you have to realise the Divine. Out of the four kinds of seekers, the most supreme is the wise one who is realising their cosmic consciousness. The experiencer and the experience are one; this whole reality is woven together like beads on a mala. So where is the Divine? It is within you and without you, it is everywhere. We live in the mother and the mother lives in us. The formless is showing up in all forms. All forms are the forms of the Divine. All forms are forms of consciousness of that supreme being. The presence of that intelligence is very evident in everything you experience. It is important to understand it at the level of your intellect, experience it at the level of your heart and wake up to it at the level of your soul. This is the profound, elegant teaching.

Now since all forms are ultimately forms of the formless, then all forms represent a fundamental doorway into that infinite value. No form exists independent of other forms within the field and this interconnectedness of reality is not just on the level of formless. It is also on the level of form. Even the body is made up of borrowed parts which have accumulated a certain level of organisation. As the body is born, it starts to consume and that consumption, that interaction with the planet, starts to create a structure which grows. For there to be a tree, there has to be a connection with the tree-ness of the tree. It is a fundamental fact of life. So one has to embody this interconnectedness of being for it is that one consciousness that pervades through all that is manifest and unmanifest. All form arises through the interconnectedness of being. All structures arise through the interconnectedness of being. No structure exists independently, on its own.

Now when one really understands this, one realises the scope of influence that one has. For reality responds to our consciousness state because the reality you see and observe around you is an extension of Self even on the level of matter. All matter is organised within that one field. The material cause of all matter exists independently in that interconnected field of that particular structure. So as long as there is a certain level of energy within the body, the atoms within the body organise in a certain manner which we can identify as a human body. At the moment of the clinical death of the body, as the life force starts to be less cognizable within it, it starts to dissolve into its material cause. The atoms are no longer organised in that certain manner. They start to be organised in a different manner and so you find that even on the level of the physical body, there is

On Realising the Self

interconnectedness of being. There is that infinite field of conscious energy that permeates the entire reality. As you realise this fact, there is a revolution in the way you live, a revolution in the way you perceive and interact with this living reality. This is an invitation to really look, to contemplate, to observe what our relationship to reality is, what our relationship to that intelligence is, that creative principle, that sustaining principle, that dissolving principle.

This teaching is of the cosmic nature of reality, the brilliance of this fundamental truth about reality. If you don't embody and apply the teaching at the level of your own being, you remain on the surface at the level of thought. It is important that you really use the wisdom and apply it. Contemplate it. Dive deep into it and start to fundamentally alter the way you walk through this life. It is very easy to forget. It is very easy to get lost in the theatre of life, in the feature film that's playing on the big screen, and become totally oblivious to the screen. When you go to the cinema to watch a movie, it plays out on the screen, the scenes change, the characters come and go but the screen remains the same. It is quite natural therefore, that when you watch the movie, you forget there is a screen there. If you remember and think about the screen while you are watching it, if that is what is dominating, then you are not able to enjoy the movie. At the subtler level of your understanding, you know that there is a screen and that is why when the movie finishes you are able to leave the cinema, the life of the movie is over. In the human lifespan of the body, it is very natural to get totally absorbed and become oblivious to the fundamental truth of what is going on. When one finds oneself surrounded by constant drama, an absence of interconnectedness of being occurs, an absence of unity, and then only separation dominates.

Lesson 8
On a Life of Love

It is good to ask the questions, but we must have the capacity to understand and receive the answers. What is the imperishable, transcendent reality? It is potential, pure potential, transcendent of all dynamism; the profound field of stillness. Within this deepest womb, there is the cosmic Om, the cosmic vibration. That pulsation itself has a cosmic nature and is interconnected with all, there is no gap. That pulsation holds the profound stillness, there is no dynamism. Now without vibration there is nothing. So we live in a vibratory universe; nothing is static, there is only dynamism. There is nothing still in the universe, just events unfolding at different rates. The universe itself is an event and though all these events are unfolding within that interconnected vibratory field which has no boundaries, this field of energy, the Divine Mother, modifies itself into the soul, the individualized expression.

Spirit is what gives birth to plurality, to multiplicity. The infinite manifesting as the finite, the soul, is that power which manifests the dream, then becomes the dream and then becomes every character in the dream. It manifests through its own power as different individuals in the dream and then every individual in the dream has a full body, characteristics and certain attributes. So the whole dreamscape, that whole manifest reality, is created through that force, that supreme potential. Then comes the pulsation, plurality, the cosmic play. That pulsation is the cosmic mother principle. The moment that pulsation arises from there, there are further modifications; spontaneous creativity starts to arise from this dimension. But there is that transcendent ground which is at the absolute level, the subtlest level, where there is no pulsation which form first requires; the infinite requires that field to create any finite form.

Within the higher Self lies the domain of the manifest reality. The manifest reality is interconnected; there are no boundaries at any level. Boundaries are nothing but a level of perception, that is all. The boundaries are perceived by our nervous system. So within that pulsatory field that further modifies itself into the soul, the individual, that which sets all this in motion is the cosmic action, Om. It is the principle that sets this process in motion. Om is inherent within the pulsation. That's why Om has three values to it: ah oh mmmm. The three aspects of the flow within time: the generative principle, the organising principle and the destructive principle. The beginning, middle and end. Everything that comes into existence is maintained in existence and then dissolves from existence. It is generated, organised and destroyed. These are all values within the pulsation, that vibratory play of consciousness that allows the dreamer to dream all this into existence while still remaining in cosmic stillness. The beauty of it is that the stillness still remains. The stillness does not lose its stillness when this pulsation arises. Stillness remains, yet dynamism arises. That dynamism does not arise in bits and pieces, it's not random. There is an elegance in it. It rises as a whole; that vibratory field rises as a whole. It does not arise as one action here and then one action there. The whole vibratory field rises simultaneously; the fabric of the unified field, the interconnectedness, is whole. And this unified field which further modifies itself into the soul is deathless, yet it experiences birth and death. That is why the question, "What happens when I die?" becomes irrelevant because death is an experience as love is an experience. These experiences have a distinct effect, just as enlightenment is an experience, and they have different values within the being. You are born through the universe; you don't come into it. If you came into the universe, then where were you before? No, you come through the universe; all forms require the vibratory universe. If this pulsation is not there, no form can be there, for form requires limitation and limitation can only be born out of vibration.

This pulsation is intelligence, is the intelligent cause. The material and the intelligent cause are in this pulsation. There is intelligence in the field itself and that field is what organises from the inside out. As a cell is organised from the inside out, the atom is organised from the inside out. There is no one coming from the outside, the universe is being organised from the inside, from the source. Its organising structures are within itself. All of it is happening within the field of consciousness. The astral field is the domain of celestial values. What is the celestial value? It is where the laws of nature are slightly different.

The vibration is different. Your body appears at a certain level because of a certain vibration which organises matter in a certain form and that form holds as long as that vibratory field is there. When you die, life starts to draw away. The energy that gives that structure to the body is drawn away and so it starts to disintegrate. The form finds a simpler expression. Self-generation of energy is no longer there. That is death.

In the celestial realm, there are laws but they are different just like in a dream where different laws apply. There are specific laws in the dream world which are very distinct from the five-sensory, waking world. Time behaves differently. In that celestial realm, the forms are maintained within that field but these forms and the laws of nature differ. The forms are not like the grosser bodies of this realm where we exist through the power of illusion. The energetic field of the life force is still there, still organising a certain level of memory, of I am-ness, of understanding. Like when you are in a dream, it has a certain reality within it and there is an energy being used in its generation. So if you have a really terrifying dream, you wake feeling exhausted but if you have celestial dreams, then you wake up cheerful. In the astral realm the body, the individualized soul, has a certain level of structure, of cognition. How is that possible? Within the soul is the field that generates that structure, not the other way round. That is why when the body dies within the vibratory field, it disintegrates but that happens only at the grosser level, in the five-sensory physical reality. It also manifests at the astral level which has a certain level of similarity but there are distinctions.

The subtlest value of the soul is awareness; for within the deepest level of being is the supreme, creative spirit, the ultimate observer. On this planet you see human beings at different states of consciousness, different levels of evolution. There are beings at denser states and there are beings at elevated states. Similarly, in astral realms there are beings at denser states and beings at elevated states with a greater state of elegance, greater state of unity. It's all within the field of consciousness, within the dream of the Divine. Death is certain although most live in denial about this. They live as if they are going to live eternally as this body but the eternal part of us is not the body and has to be located and discovered. When one dies, one goes where one is in one's most consistent consciousness state. So those whose minds are fixed on the celestial value of Self find that in death. For the whole of life is the preparation for death; you die as you live. Death is the culmination of the life you've lived so if you are moving in the direction of self-discovery, then death becomes celebratory. Those who are not moving in the direction of Self-discovery will discover whatever thought structures they have been creating and are most absorbed in. If they are just nasty to other people all day, complaining, gossiping, being unkind and ungrateful, then they die with that level of consciousness. If one is evolving and journeying in the direction of one's essential nature, is engaged in evolution, then death is just a progression of that experience. For death is nothing but an experience within the field of awareness of the soul. So we should not waste this life; one should live fearlessly but with great wisdom. There is a preciousness to life; we should make life count so our death can be meaningful. Death can only be meaningful if life is meaningful. Life and death are inseparable from each other. There is no fear in death when you see your true Self as deathless. You will experience yourself as deathless if you have lived generously with a grateful heart and with compassion. At the point of death, draw your energy up, focus at the third eye, and be absorbed in the breathless state, for death is the breathless state. So, through our meditation and kriya we can micro-dose death. We are training ourselves to die in an elegant manner.

The soul is not sitting somewhere inside the body like a truck driver driving a truck. If that was the case, then changes to the truck, changes to the mechanisms of the truck, would not affect the truck driver at all. But when you work with the body, not just on the physical level but on the level of energy, on the level of the subtler dimensions of being, there is a certain effect that starts to happen within the consciousness state. That is an important understanding for us to grasp. We are not just the body; we are expressing as the body and expressing as the life force. We are expressing as the heart and we are expressing as the mind. So all these values have to be refined and addressed in an integrated approach; we must address all the different aspects of being. A certain level of love and devotion is required, for right action which is not accompanied with a sense of reverence within the heart can lead one to the spiritual ego. It is of paramount importance to cultivate that deep reverential heart filled with love. We see the arrogance of the self-righteous ego, where individuals take on a certain behaviour and believe themselves to be superior to others. This is not the path.

This is an invitation to live that life of deep awareness. The one who is embodying those values, the one who is progressing in that state, the one who is not just on the level of the word but is able to go to the deepest value, those beings who have gained self-awareness to that degree, who have gained a certain level of unity within themselves beyond cosmic, these are the individuals who become free from the compulsion of the cycle of birth and death. The freedom from the cycle of birth and death is attained when you realise who you are, your true Self. When you wake up, you become free from the dream state. When the soul is totally unaware of its own soul nature, when the self is unaware of its own Self nature, it is only aware of itself as this mind-body-ego apparatus, then it is constantly stuck in this birth and death, birth and death, birth and death struggle through life. Because when it is reborn, it has to learn everything all over again. It struggles. It is helpless. It has a certain level of astral memory and then starts to forget everything.

With the dropping of the body, there is a certain level of experience which dawns in every soul of their own soul nature. But as the cycle continues, that memory fades and one starts all over again. This is the delusion of birth and death. Like when you awaken from a dream, the dream lingers on a little in your mind and then you forget. You sleep, you dream, you wake, you sleep, you dream, you wake, this cycle repeats over and over again. You are born and you die but when you realise your true Self, you become aware of your own deathless nature. The freedom from death is you becoming aware of your own deathless nature. When you become aware of your true nature, your timelessness, that is the freedom from time. Then you can exist in time, cosmic consciousness becomes stable; the body drops and cosmic consciousness remains. Instead of being propelled by the ever-repeating cycle, awareness remains intact. When the birth cycles are in alignment with the vibratory field that you are maintaining most consistently, then the birth is not a compulsion but rather a privilege. It's not happening to you but for you, through you. That is the state of freedom from birth and death; freedom from this cycle of birth and death is the freedom from ignorance. Many tend to think of death as leaving this planet, going somewhere else, it's never here, always there. It is an escapist theory to never be here, always be somewhere else. That is not this teaching; the teaching is very clear. The cycle of birth and death is within the consciousness field and if you are not aware of your own essential nature, then you remain forever stuck within the cycle of birth and death for heaven and hell are of one's own making. If one is ignorant, then one remains unaware. One thinks one is free, but one is enslaved by the shackles of conditioning.

This life is the expression of the Divine, cosmic consciousness; this is not a curse. The freedom from birth and death does not mean there is something wrong with being here. The truth is, you will always be here; wherever you are, here you will be. In context to you, the only location is here. Here is the play of the Divine, the play of supreme consciousness. This is a sweet dream. If one is living a life of evolution, then one looks forward to death as one looks forward to every moment, to every day, knowing any day might be the day of your passing.

So freedom from birth and death is gained by those who are able to cognize their own soul nature, their own timeless nature. As you begin to cognize your own timeless nature, you start gaining freedom from birth and death, meaning that you are aware of the cycle of birth and death happening instead of being within the cycle of birth and death. If one is living supremely, then death is just a continuation. A whole new sensory experience becomes available in death and is to be welcomed but not because one hates being here and is looking towards death as a respite; there is no respite in death. Death is just an altered experience being experienced by the experiencer. Where are the different dimensions of reality? Here. Not somewhere out there. Parallel universes are here, just vibrating at a slightly different frequency. For only from the timeless can time emerge. It's cycles within cycles within cycles. If one is aware, then one can enjoy this whole play as the cycles of time continue. When one starts to awaken to one's own essential nature, then one finds these movements are within oneself and one can enjoy the whole show.

There is another dimension which is beyond the infinity of the universe. That dimension is the dimension expressing as the universe but it is also the cause of the universe. The cause of the universe is the dimension which is unchanging. That unchanging dimension of being, the transcendent, pure, no-movement dimension rises up. It is subtler than the infinity of the universe; it is the dimension of the changeless being. That changeless, timeless being is infinite. It has to be infinite because the concept of space-time does not exist at that level.

For there to be the infinite, there has to be a finite. This is pure, concept-less, and when one goes to that deeper level, makes contact with that changeless dimension of reality, that is the absolute oneness. As one is aware of that and is able to experience that, then one is experiencing the infinite cycles of the universes. Once the soul becomes aware of this dimension, then irrespective of which dimension in the manifest reality one is in, one is living that enlightenment, one is living that supreme consciousness state.

With all this intellectual knowledge, there is still a need for devotion, for love, because without love, without that state of devotion, nothing is possible. Devotion is what makes us receptive. That love, that devotion, gives us the quality of natural mindfulness and our resistance drops. A devotee is always in remembrance of the object of their devotion, it is constantly there. That is the beauty of love. When we are devoted to truth, we are devoted to realising our own true nature; we are engaging in the practice. We are integrating that knowledge but we are also in love with the whole thing. Then it naturally rises up in our relative reality. Even though our conditioning still comes up every now and then and creates opposition, we are in love with the whole awakening. It's such an incredible thing. It naturally corrects and wipes out the glitches. Even though we might lose our way now and then, we will not be lost for too long. That is the beauty of devotion, of cultivating that heart full of love, full of compassion, full of appreciation. That is why the heart is the seat of cosmic consciousness.

On a Life of Love

Those who are practising and raising their consciousness, raising their energy, awakening that infinite potential of being, raising the value of light, the light of consciousness, the light of being, find liberation. And liberation is the nature of Self. The self is liberated but the self is also not liberated. Both values of self are correct. The Self at the deepest level is totally liberated; at the relative level, it has learning still to do. As one engages in the integrated practice, refining the intellect, making contact with the knowledge through deep, still meditation, engaging in the subtler practices, drawing the energy up, moving consistently to the third eye, aligning and awakening, that golden current begins to attain Self-awareness in life and in death. For as in life, so in death. This is important to understand. The evolution of the individual is a personal endeavour. It is not an accident that happens to you; evolution of the self within the relative field of reality is not accidental. So the value of the increasing light within is the energy rising, illuminating all. The way of the light and the dark is eternal and as long as there is light, there is going to be darkness. As long as there is darkness, there will be light. For there to be an experience of darkness, there has to be an experience of light. For there to be the experience of absence, there has to be the possibility of presence. If there is no presence, there can be no absence. Darkness is just the absence of light; it is not in opposition to light. All light is an experience within the context of varying degrees of light. If there is a uniformity of light in all directions, then there would be no experience of light within our own system. For there to be an experience of light, there has to be the experience of darkness. If it were sunny all the time, you would have no concept of sunny. For you to know what it is to be sunny, you have to know what it is not to be sunny. Light and dark are eternal and in the relative field of reality, duality will persist eternally.

Lesson 9

On Unlocking the Secrets Within

As we evolve, we become more receptive. The tendency within one to feed on negativity, to be attached to negativity within oneself and everyone else, is prevalent when the lower mind is dominating, for the tendency of the lower mind is to constantly move in the direction of that which is not there. When one is in a state, one will always focus on the negative aspects. But when we transcend this tendency and start to focus more on the bigger picture instead of just remaining attached to the problem or that which is missing, then we are expanding and more receptive. Secrets are kept within traditions, within teachings, because they require a certain level of maturity. Because the word secret is being used in this lesson, one has to approach it with a certain level of maturity, a deep sense of responsibility, of reverence, realising how powerful it is so that one does not dilute it, cheapen it, misquote and misuse the knowledge to spread it incorrectly. You have to value it.

The fundamental cause of suffering is incorrect knowledge. When you know the root of an issue is incorrect knowledge, then you can do something about it. You can learn and change, for it is wisdom that frees you. The fundamental cause of suffering is because you do not fully understand. These secrets are keys which open doors but they are only helpful if you use them; a key is only of use when you open the door. If you just keep it in your pocket and walk around feeling special because you have a secret, then there is no evolution. You remain the same person. When one experiences growth, then one is ready to be awakened to a deeper level of knowing. Many of us come to this desire for answers from a place of crisis. We may be struggling in the beginning, in a state of despondency but as we evolve and grow, we want to learn from a place of passion, a place of devotion, a place of love, not from a place of doubt anymore. We need to grow in order to understand.

Once one starts to understand, starts to gain wisdom, then the knowledge itself is enjoyable. That is the bliss of wisdom, this is the radiance of knowledge, true knowledge. When the light of true knowledge starts to arise in you, there is immense bliss in that knowledge. That knowledge is liberating and as one perceives that knowledge, then it naturally flows. The entire manifest reality is permeated by the Divine, cosmic consciousness, as ice is by water. All beings dwell within that consciousness, but they are not that consciousness. The beauty of wisdom is that it requires a deep level of understanding and there are different ways of understanding it. First on the level of the soul but the soul has to gain its supreme Self value through awareness. Everything that you experience, all that exists, is within the field of supreme consciousness. When you truly go within, you realise that within disappears; that is cosmic consciousness, within and without merge. It is impossible for the experiencer to experience something without their awareness absorbing that. The experiencer's awareness is what gives experience validity. The experience comes alive only when the awareness of the individual makes contact with it. All beings dwell within cosmic consciousness, the individualized soul, the elemental reality, the great spirit, the Absolute, all are within one. Dimensions within dimensions within dimensions. At the ultimate level, it is all permeated by that one consciousness, indivisible in its essential nature. No finite value can claim infinity just for itself.

So no one can claim the copyright on totality. From the point of view of awareness, this is a helpful clue into understanding that the roles that you play are all within you; you are not the role. From the point of view of infinity, limited boundaries do not exist. All beings are modifications of that one consciousness but no one value within the finite expression can claim infinity to itself, in isolation. If you want to go looking for yourself, you have to move in the direction of Self. For you to begin to realise yourself, you have to understand you're not in the world, the world is in you. That is cosmic consciousness. Once you begin to understand that, then you come to that level where you are in the world and the world is within you. And all beings that exist within that consciousness remain forever. All memories, all shapes and forms are constructed within that field of consciousness. So when we observe the universe, we see it has a certain level of memory.

When you look at a seed, the emptiness within it holds the design of the tree. The design of the tree is within that seed of the tree because there is a certain mechanism already inherent in nature which when activated results in a specific expression that is distinct from another seed. On breaking the seed open, you don't really find much in there. Yet there is a code within that turns this seed into that tree; this memory remains forever. As the divine consciousness expresses as the soul within the higher Self, within space-time, one is gaining greater and greater unity and the memories are maintained within that. As one gains unity consciousness, the particular experiences that one has are still maintained at that level of being. The gaining of unity, of wisdom, is maintained even when the body dissolves; the form changes but this elegance is maintained within the womb of the universe, within the womb of the spirit, for it is infinite. When the soul realises this, that is a divine life. A divine life is that which is cognizing its own divine nature.

Spirit dwells in everything, in the finite and the infinite. All sentient and non-sentient beings are expressions of a pulsation of consciousness. So one can see the river as an extension of oneself, one can see the mountain as an extension of oneself, the sun, the bird and so on. Nothing is inert, everything is pulsating and shining with spirit. Within the tree there is spirit. There is an energetic intelligence within a crystal, an energetic intelligence within the plant and the river. Keeping that awareness, that knowledge within your own being is the Divine gaining more and more of its own divinity, the human gaining more and more of its own divinity.

One doesn't have to lose infinity to gain infinity; one can remain infinite while honouring the finite. One can remain in the transcendent, that ground of being, while honouring one's own individual soul's journey; maintaining that cosmic consciousness but also remaining as the soul, within the manifest reality. For all knowledge is knowledge of the Self, the cosmic Self; that is all that exists. This is a very integrated approach to the teaching which requires a very mature understanding. And maturity is a dynamic phenomenon just as enlightenment is a dynamic phenomenon.

There are always those who are not able to understand the teachings but it is not that they cannot understand the teachings or the teacher or the world outside, it is that they are not able to understand themselves. The root of ignorance is within each and every individual. The ignorant are confused by their own self and so not able to understand the teachings. The soul identified with ignorance is unable to recognise the truth so keeps projecting that into the relative field of reality. The Divine is embedded in every expression of life, sentient and non-sentient, so the issue is not with the sacred. The issue is with the idea of what sacred is and that idea is born from the consciousness state of the generator of the idea. There is a tendency for human beings to remain engulfed by their own ignorance and then to project that ignorance all around themselves, including on their idea of the Divine.

Those individuals bewildered by their own ignorance get so deeply attached to that ignorance that they align themselves to their own dark, demonic nature. Within the relative field of reality, duality is the law. Within each and every one of us is the Buddha and also our greatest enemy; this is an important thing to understand. The demon is not hiding in hell but rather it is hiding within each and every one of us. So if the individual remains in this grip of ignorance, there comes a time when they find the ego identity dominating the soul completely. Based on this conditioned, isolated identity, the individual then generates a lot of incorrect knowledge all around themself, finding confirmation and support in others with similar, ignorant viewpoints, generating a strong level of arrogance. And this arrogance based on absolutely incorrect knowledge gives the individual a certain strength; they rise up stronger than individuals who are in the middle, who are perplexed. Those arrogant individuals become very charming because they seem to be very confident, very certain in their point of view. This power is based on keeping others weak.

Those individuals, deluded by their own ignorance, identify and align themselves with their own evil nature. There is no evil inherent, just ignorant souls. It is a very important point to understand; one cannot transcend what one does not acknowledge. One has to acknowledge one's own ability for violence, for hypocrisy, for arrogance, for what one does not acknowledge, one cannot transcend. If the individual is not being educated in the direction of developing their own sovereignty, diving deep within their own being, then they are prone to be swept in the direction of a stronger energy. What is the law of nature? In any situation, whoever has a stronger energy will prevail. So this tendency of getting possessed by a certain point of view gives an individual a greater energy compared to the individuals who act like they are a deer caught in the headlights. So engage in evolution, for when you are scattered you are weak within yourself. When you are weak within yourself, you feel powerless and a soft target for the lower tendencies. For one to be manipulated, one has to first agree to be manipulated, consciously or unconsciously. One who does not agree to be manipulated cannot be manipulated because you cannot be manipulated without your own consent. You are a sovereign being. You are the infinite expressing as the finite. You are cosmic consciousness incarnate. How can you be manipulated without your own consent?

Those who are actively engaged in realising their higher Self find liberation. If one isolates devotion from wisdom, it becomes dogma and that is not the true devotion. This is not some passive surrender; it is a dynamic surrender. As one dives deep within the depth of great wisdom, refines one's intellect, works with one's energy, one realises that the mystery holds, for there will always be a certain level of mystery. The relevant knowledge will flow through the individual as they gain a greater and greater value but there will always be a certain level of mystery within the manifest reality, a certain level of the unknown. When the devotion is alive, the individual begins to cognize that great mystery; when that pain arises in the relative field of reality, one has to be able to observe that and then one is actively able to surrender it to the sacred. That active surrender is liberating and that pain starts to be transformed through love. Faith is not a cover-up for fear; faith is an extension of one's loving awareness. It is one's capacity to be at ease in the presence of the unknown. What keeps the game interesting is the realisation of the limitation of one's intellect. That even though one is evolving and refining, there will still be things which will always remain mysterious.

This ability for one to dive deep and recognise that sacred dimension within one's own being, engage in this field of diversity and still be with spirit, gives one courage to face this reality, this pain, and to love. For in this manifest reality, bodies are born and bodies die; they enter our heart, we interact with them, we experience love and connection and develop a certain level of appreciation for that person, that form. When that person is no longer locatable in that form, naturally there is pain but if you don't see this as the play of the Divine, then the whole process of life becomes excruciating. You become scared of life, scared of loving, scared of losing. You develop this vocabulary of losing and loss and by the end of your life, you have lost a lot, even though you came naked and with nothing into this life, somehow you have lost so much by the end, it's a life of losses. But that pain is the beauty of love. There is nothing wrong with that. It increases your capacity to love; that pain does not turn into misery, into sourness. It turns into a deeper state of appreciation, a deeper silence, deeper compassion. For love and wisdom are inseparable.

So devotion, that surrender, is not a passive surrender. This is not some kind of dogma. This realisation of the sacred is an essential value, knowing and understanding the impermanence of all things. The individual surrenders and discovers the supreme spirit, then sails across this ocean of life effortlessly, all through developing inner cognition, insight, silence, love. The one who is supremely wise, able to engage intellectually and innocently surrender, is able to let go. They are able to be in awe, to be humble, to have the courage to love while still knowing they will experience a certain level of pain. The presence of pain is in every life as is the presence of beauty; the presence of grace is in every life as is the presence of mystery. When you can truly understand that, then compassion is born. But for compassion to be born, there has to be that inner vitality, that strong sacred energy, that spirit. Otherwise, you are overwhelmed by the waves of pain and life becomes an emotional melodrama. The truth is life is impermanent. All shapes and forms dissolve, people you love and who are brilliant, who are kind and generous, all disappear within the relative field of reality, they are no longer locatable in this realm. But you come into this life naked and with nothing so you don't lose anything, you only gain.

The soul's eternal journey is a journey in this realm and beyond, experiencing the nectar of the earthly life and the nectar of the astral life. Depending on one's longing, one will keep finding what one is looking for because one experiences these realms based on one's own consciousness. One is awareness so all experiences are within one's awareness and one can only evolve here. Spirit is everywhere. Your higher Self is within you but it's not going to be obvious unless you want it to be. You still have the liberty to deny that experience but that does not keep love from loving you. Even when you are in denial of that, love is still loving you. The Divine is present equally in all beings but only those who are willing to recognise that have it revealed to them. This is the nature of spirit, the nature of the Absolute. Infinity is present within you and all around but for it to be revealed to you, you have to be willing for it to be revealed and ready to move in that direction. Just because you have not seen it and you remain isolated in your own consciousness field unable to cognize it, that does not mean that it doesn't exist. It will still exist. But it will only be revealed to those who are devoted, those who are consistent and sincere within their own realisation. The spirit is always whispering messages of love but you have to learn to listen. In order to be able to listen, you have to be silent within yourself. If you are too busy listening to your own thoughts, you are not silent and then you cannot hear.

When one awakens, one begins to see how much love has always been in one's life. There has never been a moment where there has not been love, for the nature of Self is love. All love is directed towards Self. Love knows one thing only and that is to love. This is a love which is at the fundamental fabric of existence. And when you are thriving, when you are experiencing that love, when you are really experiencing the sacred nature of your life and reality, then you find forgiveness is natural. It is the intelligent move. It's as natural for you to forgive as it is for the rose to emanate a fragrance. If you remain in that same consciousness state where you have felt hurt, then you just walk around angry and even if you think you have forgiven, you have not. You have just suppressed it, trying to convince yourself but secretly you hold an agenda and project it into your world, your reality of life. To forgive requires you raising your status. So here, in that field of supreme being, there is no judgement. There is only love; cause and effect. You put your hand into the fire, you will get burnt. That has nothing to do with the fire having anything against you. It is just the nature of fire. So too, when you start to do the work which is required, if you are willing to grow, you will discover the Divine, for that love is present everywhere. If the Divine is present everywhere, equally and unconditionally, then the experience of it is only dependent on the experiencer. Each and every one of us can access that. For that state of love and devotion and surrender gives one courage.

Lesson 10
On Discovering the Excellent

When one has awakened to that deeper level of listening, that deeper knowingness, one generates a certain capacity to understand, a certain consciousness state. For somebody who does not have that consciousness state, this here and now has no meaning. So one has to awaken to a deeper level of knowing within oneself to have access to the brilliance that is being here. This is an invitation to rise up to your own greatness. This science requires that the knower go through a fundamental shift. If the knower does not go through a fundamental shift, then the knowing cannot arise. It is important to realise that knowledge is relevant in proportion to the relevance of the knower and if the knower does not evolve, the knowledge is not evolutionary. It's just information and that information can be used in all kinds of destructive, manipulative ways. So the knower has to evolve for the knowledge to evolve. As the knower goes through the shift, the knowing goes through the shift too. The potential of the knowledge remains unrealised if one does not evolve.

On Discovering the Excellent   143

If the knower does not evolve, then they are bound to misunderstand, misappropriate and misuse the knowledge.

So this is an invitation to practise and transform, an invitation to a way of life, refining and awakening; it is an invitation to a journey of Self-realisation. Knowledge is endless and so too is ignorance; there is no end to misunderstanding. There is infinity in both directions. Even the great sages forget; even the great maharishis and celestial beings do not fully grasp all of this. As long as there is someone, there is something to learn. For there to be localised consciousness, a soul, there has to be a certain level of ignorance, a certain level of forgetfulness. For there to be any individual value of the finite rising within space-time, there has to be, on the part of the individual value, a certain level of ignorance, of forgetfulness. So as long as there is any finite value locatable within the manifest realm, and that can be within the earth or the celestial realms, then one cannot claim to have the absolute truth. No one who exists can totally grasp it all; they can realise their higher Self and cognize the Absolute but they do not fully know.

The dance goes on. As long as there is form, as long as there is someone, there is something to be learned. The moment everything is known within the finite value, then that finite value gains infinite value and there is no form, no location, anymore. They are not locatable in any dimension. It is part of that timeless, transcendent ground of being. In the celestial realms, in the earthly realms, there can be that illuminated state but that illuminated state is not a full stop because if you claim you know everything, then you are stuck in the ever-repeating known. No one who exists fully grasps the Absolute, for the moment the individualized value fully grasps it, it ceases to be. The structure cannot hold, it dissolves and is non-locatable. That level of forgetfulness has to be inherent within the manifestation process. For that indivisible whole to rise up within the realm of plurality, to play a role within the field of relativity, it has to have a certain level of investment in its modified nature. If it doesn't have investment in its modified nature, then the play cannot go on.

For one to realise oneself, one has to generate that intensity within and as one generates that intensity the Divine starts to rise. You begin to locate the sacred, that spirit, the infinite potential within you, your own higher Self, as an intense experience. The lion of freedom starts to roar inside of you. The Himalaya of your own being starts to shine bright within you as you realise your own excellence, your own higher Self. For at the heart of every experience is brilliance, is love, even the most painful of experiences. When you become present with that, you will find something truly precious. Go to the heart because if we remain on the periphery of the experience we won't find the Himalaya, we won't find the lion, we won't find the diamond. There is a diamond within every experience, even in the experiences we do not prefer. That is the nature of life. Not all the experiences that will pass through our awareness will be something we like, but if we learn to adapt to them, then the pain becomes a great teaching. For when you go to the heart, you find unity. When you meet those challenging experiences with a meditative awareness, you will find the jewel shining back. There is excellence

On Discovering the Excellent 145

waiting to be discovered in every experience. There is brilliance waiting to be discovered in every experience. Your life starts to rise up. You keep discovering the extraordinary because you are developing that ability and attuning yourself to it. Then you will keep stumbling into the extraordinary which is hiding within every ordinary experience. That infinite potential within each and every one of us, the potential for excellence, the experience of brilliance, is the experience of our highest Self. That is self-respect; that is self-love.

We are designed to be in ecstasy. We are designed to move in the direction of excellence, of brilliance. Our minds are designed to learn. Our being is designed to move in the direction of greater and greater states of knowing and all these movements are in the direction of Self. All love is directed toward Self. All this seeking is in the direction of spirit, the higher Self, the Divine within. The different aspects of excellence within different spheres are something which we should be aware of. For each and every one of us is designed for excellence, not excellence to be measured by some external authority but excellence realised by one's own Self. The true measure of excellence is the experiencer's state of fulfilment, the experiencer's state of thriving. We should not spend our time here living in some kind of waiting room, in fear, in denial of the inevitable. We are designed to evolve. And so, even though the cosmic consciousness that expresses in all aspects is everywhere, to realise one's own nature and evolve requires a deep self-respect, a deep worthiness, a recognition of our own capacity to excel, for the realisation of our own spirit nature is the highest form of excellence. That which is the most magnificent of all manifestation is also the potential of our own inner being. It is the potential of our own nature. For that potential to become expressed in reality, it has to be known. Then that brilliance naturally raises the status of the individual in their own eyes and in their interaction with the relative field of reality.

So it is a dual movement. One has to accept where one is. One has to honour one's journey. One has to embrace where one is but at the same time, one must hold oneself accountable. As there is the banyan tree to the shrub, there is that brilliance on the level of the unmanifest and the manifest within each and every one of us. But in order to discover that, one has to become radically open to that possibility. The moment one does, that in itself is great self-respect, great self-love. One has to be committed to that excellence within. And this commitment is not merely an idea. One has to realise that one is designed to discover the extraordinary, is designed to excel; the soul is designed to excel. Because the soul is the Divine and the nature of the Divine is excellence, is brilliance, and that is the nature of each and every one of us. So the excellence that is there has to be activated, otherwise it remains an unrealised potential and that unrealised potential haunts you. When you know you have not done your best, you know you have not given it your all, it haunts you. This stable confidence cannot just arise by fooling oneself. It arises by dedication and discovery of one's own excellence and when one shows up for one's own Self that is the highest of the highest. Then your brain naturally starts to get filled with more energy and greater clarity, there is more bliss floating within your system. There is a strength and stability, an openness at the heart. This is the nature of you awakening to your own sacred Self.

This is a practice, a dedication. This teaching says that the Divine lives within and also in the brilliance that is reflected out. This is the teaching of unity. That brilliance is within every expression of life and every experience. There is the sacred in every experience but it has to be discovered. You have to dive deep to bring up the pearl. If you remain just on the surface, then you cannot live a brilliant life. So go to the heart of every experience and go to your own heart to discover your own brilliance. Be dedicated to your excellence in any activity that you do because you deserve your best and as long as you're not willing to give your best to yourself, then your light does not rise to its full potential. Be ready to sacrifice your lower tendencies and this excellent life, the life which is filled with brilliance not based on somebody else's opinion, is yours. Nobody else gets to take away the sacred from you. You get to decide. No theory gets to reduce this magnificent reality. You decide what universe you want to live in. For the nature of your deepest Self is brilliance. You are designed to be brilliant. And when you engage in any relative activity, engage in it as a meditation. Be exemplary. Go to the heart of the activity. Even if it is just you walking or sitting by the river or looking at the moon. Learn to go to the heart. What you feed into the system, the system feeds back to you. What you feed into the great infinite, the infinite feeds back to you. It is a feedback loop.

The beauty of wisdom is that when it rises in you, you do not take ownership of it, that wisdom is just rising up. If you're truly wise, your idea of ownership lessens. For excellence to truly liberate you, there has to be no ownership of it. The ego has to learn to not take ownership of it, then the excellence just flows. The less one does, the more that happens. That does not mean one does not engage. One engages but the brilliance is flowing, it takes over and you become that great field of unity, that timelessness, extending out into space-time and expressing itself without hesitation. As you awaken your own infinite potential, the brilliance in you, you will naturally become an exemplary inspiration. You are in wonder, in awe, instead of this chronic boredom which is the ego-mind state. You realise the incredible vastness of this. The form is infinite and the formless is infinite. Within the dimension of form, there is infinity. Within the formless, there is infinity. Infinity in all directions, no end to the glory of being.

Lesson 11
On Seeing and Believing

If knowledge comes alive in you, then there is bound to be an alchemy, a transformation which has to happen and we see that transformation happening as we evolve. The questions change to those of a seeker who is understanding; they are of a different value, a different nature. The hallmarks of the wise one are deep reverence and gratefulness because the presence of gratefulness opens the doorway to wisdom. Wherever there is gratefulness, love will arise, delusion is wiped out through that gratitude. That deep gratefulness that arises is liberating, one is no longer bound by the delusion anymore. When one has transcended the crisis state and is in the state is of equanimous exploration, there is a state of surrender. The unsurrendered, the ignorant, are not really looking for an answer to their questions. They already have an answer in their mind and are looking for confirmation of that. If they don't receive that particular answer which is already in their mind, they feel threatened; within the ignorant ego-mind, it is a challenge. When one hears the answers to one's questions and embodies them and applies them, one is in the state of surrendered inquisitiveness which raises one's deserving power. But the evolution of the soul has to be a gradual unfoldment. That is the sustainable enlightenment, one which gradually unfolds. Anybody looking for a quick fix, one secret technique, one magic pill, will be disappointed. This is not a quick fix. It requires the illumination which is stable, not just a one-off; it is a consistent, gradual unfoldment, an evolutionary journey. If one wants to truly progress then one has to commit to it for life. You show up, you remain consistent, you have room for all that arises.

The entire creation of all that is, is within the Divine, that Absolute; all that moves and all that doesn't move. But it is not just seen, it is known; it is a consciousness state. What we call reality is a certain level of modification of reality within the certain parameter of our nervous system. Anything outside of that we are not able to perceive or experience. We cannot hear the sound frequencies above or below a certain hertz. We cannot see colours beyond a certain spectrum. For us to exist within this realm, this linear flow of time, and perceive these boundaries, this structure, requires a very specific setting for our nervous system; alteration to that setting changes the whole reality. People without the technology to naturally alter their perception might ingest psychedelics to change their view because by altering their nervous system, what they see and perceive changes. It is the modification of reality within the nervous system of the observer. A dog sees a totally different colour spectrum to us. Rats hear a totally different sound spectrum. Animals can smell a totally different universe within their sensory perception. So there is an incredible number of versions of reality and they are experienced in different ways depending on who the experiencer is and what setting the experiencer's state is at; reality modifies itself to the experiencer experiencing it.

The beauty of the human apparatus is that its setting can be altered; it is designed to be expanded. In the mundane state, the spirit remains hidden from the human. But as the human begins to refine, the seeing and that which is seen changes. As the seer alters the bandwidth of their experience, what they see will naturally change; for divine sight, one needs to alter the setting. This divine sight is not some superpower laser eyes. It is in the consciousness at the third eye. As the energy starts to rise, the experience of your own cosmic nature starts to rise up too and that which is experienced is no longer bound by the five senses. What arises is not a reality which is made up of boundaries, it is far richer. Once you can start to experience that, then you are able to exist in this material reality with a much greater elegance. You just have to have the capacity to see it, to tune yourself to that level of perception. Then as one goes deeper, phenomenal experiences start to rise within one's own consciousness; with the eyes shut one naturally still sees vivid reality far richer than by ingesting any psychedelics.

Psychedelics do not create a sustainable experience but as you cultivate certain practices, as you awaken your own inner medicine, then the transcendent experiences that start to arise don't have the side effect of regression. Instead, the side effect is progression. We are designed for this progression; if we were not, we wouldn't have that potential, that experience could not arise in us. When the energy rises up to the third eye, this cosmic vision is possible. With eyes closed, this cosmic vision, the play happening in the eternal now as the spirit, starts to reveal itself in the third eye.

When the energy moves within one's own being, one can get into that state where the expanded becomes very accessible. The infinite, multi-dimensional reality seems so present but one can then feel doubt that this is real. Why? Because when you go into that deep practice a certain level of awareness is still maintained, the I am-ness is still there. As one witnesses all this magnificent eternity unfolding in the eternal now, one can be in awe and also a little bit scared. This is a clear glimpse into the level of intensity that is the manifest reality, a total unity consciousness experience which can be phenomenally intense and magnificent but this cosmic play is also scary stuff.

The human nervous system is reductionist, it is designed to reduce reality, to see selectively, think selectively. For us to function within the human universe we have to ignore a lot, so unconsciously we delete. If you become aware of everything, all of it all at once, it becomes supremely challenging to exist. The play of emptiness unfolding itself within the consciousness state is an experience of supreme intensity, a peak of experience cognizing this manifest infinite. From the point of view of the cosmic being, the pure field of consciousness, that spirit is self-aware. We know it is self-aware because we are aware. We know we exist and from the point of view of that cosmic infinite awareness, the supreme being, it is all unfolding simultaneously and aware of it all.

On Seeing and Believing 153

Within the context of our own inner journey, we must push the parameters of what we will allow ourself to experience. But because of fear of the natural outcome of interaction with the unknown, the soul can remain absorbed in the ego-mind and stay dedicated to limitation. Our nervous system in its fundamental state is reductionist so that we are able to have a human experience. As the soul, the consciousness field, starts to expand and realise its true nature, it is no longer stuck in limitation. It is now cognizing this cosmic game in awe. But when the awareness reaches its parameter in this present consciousness state, it becomes terrified. It starts with awe and wonder, then wow, it is amazed and then terrified. What is terrifying is what the awareness has not yet met. The ability to find the wonder in the terrifying has not yet been developed. Once it has developed, that which was terrifying becomes wonderful. One's initial experience of the cosmic is awe as one is experiencing that inner ecstasy. There is awe and then it becomes terrifying.

When one understands that everything that is coming into existence dissolves, that starts to bring up fear: fear of loss, of the unknown, of annihilation. But within that experience is the possibility to learn and to see and to find invincibility, to find appreciation and to realise how incredibly, intensely precious this whole play is. Whenever you find yourself stuck, expand your awareness and catch a glimpse of the cosmic play, then all your issues will dissolve spontaneously. When you have an experience within you of this intensity, all the issues which were being generated by the lower tendencies just dissolve; they become irrelevant. You can transcend that state where the problem seemed relevant, then you realise that the problem was not really a problem. The problem existed in the consciousness state you were in; it was generating the problem. As you shift that state of mind, the problem becomes irrelevant and no longer makes any sense to you. A problem is only a problem to the state of mind experiencing it.

In the cosmic, eternal time, all the opposition is eventually destroyed; all resistance is eventually destroyed in the cosmic scheme. In the spirit realm, all potential is real but for that potential to be experienced within the individual, the individual has to act. Why should we act if it's already been resolved? For it to be real in our life, in our experience. Potentially, we are invincible but we cannot just assume it. For the potential of our invincibility to become actualized in our relative experience, we must realise it, here and now. We must act. We cannot assume our cosmic nature; we must realise it. Even though we are enlightenment, we must practise to make it a visceral reality. For only the Divine, the Absolute, exists and if only that exists, then we are that; the ultimate potential of every being that exists is the supreme realisation of their essential nature. That is total victory.

Through this cosmic third eye, when one is within that experience, time disappears. Eventually one comes out into the relative field of reality and one is a changed person but that transcendent experience does not stay forever. The memory of it remains but it has to be expressed in the relative field of reality. The vision one has is unique because the experience is only for that individual experiencing it. The Divine rises within in a unique way and one must realise the specialness, the preciousness of these experiences. In the eternal now, we have already won but in the relative field it is one step at a time; it's a living experience. When we start on the path of our own inner revolution, we are already liberated but we must keep discovering it. That is what makes it so magnificent. When we know that, then we will meet who we are. One cannot meet life as someone else. A life of invincibility has to be realised through surrendered action.

We are designed with the potential of ecstasy hiding within us but it has to be awakened within the relativity of our own experience. All that we seek we have already discovered; all that we've ever wanted is already here. The Divine is here. Infinity is here. That cosmic being is real but has to be realised; in the relative field of reality what is not realised is potentially real. When nature wants to fly, it will fly. For you to experience that flight you must step out of the nest; without that leaning in, without that trust, without that surrender, the flight will not emerge within the experience of that individual. Within every caterpillar is a potential butterfly. The caterpillar and the butterfly coexist but within the individual experience there has to be that transformation, that birth of the butterfly. That supreme fulfilment of a life, total liberation, is always there in potential. If it is not the possibility, then it can never be realised; for it to be a possibility within that unmanifest supreme field, it all has to be available now. As the consciousness state expands, it all starts to become available but one must act. That is what keeps the play interesting.

This experience unfolded within the consciousness changes everything. Once we make contact with that transcendent experience within our own being, once the veil starts to lift from our eyes, we can never be the same. When we align with this awareness, engage with the play, then we realise that everything is purposeful in our life and everything will fall into place. Even the most terrifying aspects of life are all part of that play and if one is addicted to the tendencies of the lower mind, the drama and self-destructive behaviour within oneself, then one can never see the play and one remains engulfed by it. We must step into our light regardless of any threat or attack because it's not personal. It's just the nature of the play in the relative field. As moths are attracted to the fire, similarly certain demons are attracted to our radiance. So as we start to step into our power, we have to be ready not to get suppressed by it. We need to realise that that is just a part of the journey. The attack of the demons, their opposition, overcoming the challenges are all part of the victory. It is part of our journey to realise that dimension where all of it has already been resolved.

Seeing this supreme vision as one comes into that state of greater unity, then the ability to take responsibility for one's own transgressions, conscious or unconscious, becomes available. Realisation has to accompany a sense of being ready to be forgiven. This asking for forgiveness is arising from the pure cognition of a greater truth. Having now expanded one's consciousness to the next level, one is able to stabilise and cognize the celebration that is arising within the cosmic field. It is a deep, inner realisation because one is now elevated. Filled with joy, with ecstasy, having had this experience, this move from awe to fear and then to stability and joy, this profound experience, is extremely rare. So one must hold these experiences that one has within one's own being with deep reverence, within the sanctity of one's own heart. When one has these experiences as part of becoming stable, gaining one's brilliance, one must honour them. Learn to honour the sanctity of your own inner experience. This is a very important part of our victory. As we go within ourself and have these experiences, we must cherish them and realise that these are movements of grace. We don't need to intellectualize them, decipher all the meaning, just appreciate them and honour them. Do not look for validation. Learn to own these experiences and shine. When you can own your experience within the silence of your own being, then you don't become sour.

Lesson 12

On Realising Love and Gaining Connection

There are those who realise their higher Self, the manifest reality, in an integrated manner, and then realise their essential nature beyond that as well. And there are those who are dedicated to a more aesthetic, impersonal view, withdrawing themselves. Sometimes this split is seen between devotion and knowledge, action and intellect. Knowledge finds its resolution in love and love allows the flow of knowledge. In the absence of love, knowledge is a tedious thing. Knowledge that does not naturally result in the experience of love is incomplete and love that does not move in the direction of knowledge, that does not allow knowledge to flow within, is not love. For example, to love someone is to know them. To truly love is to know deeply, it's not knowing about the person. When you know someone, you do not know about them, you know them on a deeper level. So anyone you love, you know intimately. Without the knowing, it is just an infatuation. So to love spirit, one must know spirit. To love being, one has to know being. The knowing of spirit naturally fills the heart with love and vice versa. To actively hate someone, to demonize someone, one has to not know them fully, not see them fully, for when one does, one cannot then hate them. To actively hate someone, an individual or a group, there has to be an absence of knowing. This is an important thing for us to understand.

When you know someone deeply, when you see them fully, there is the birth of compassion. When you get to know the spirit, when you get to know the transcendent experience, when you get to experience that realm within your own being, you find bliss in it. You start to find ecstasy in it. Whatever you are devoted to, you find bliss in it and that bliss is a driver of attention. It naturally draws attention to itself. So knowledge leads to devotion and devotion leads to greater knowledge. One has to move from discipline to devotion and in that devotion, when there is love flowing, one finds that the mind naturally centres on the object of one's love. What you adore captures your attention naturally. That is the state of an integrated being, a wise devotee. When you cultivate that state of devotion, you find that the resistance naturally drops. You find yourself naturally taking correct action in the direction of your evolution, in the direction of your higher Self, in the direction of spirit. Then it is not so difficult for you to move in that direction because love is the driver of attention. That which you find charming, you will have energy for. The supreme individuals are those who work with their energy, draw their attention towards their higher Self, cultivate a state of love. And this state of love naturally generates a greater knowledge. In that state, love and knowledge are not separate and the beauty of it is, the more you know, the more you love and the more you love, the more you know. So, if you want to really learn something, it will serve you to be in love with it first, to be in awe, to feel a state of connection.

When you feel a state of connection with a certain thing, you will find that the knowledge about it comes very naturally to you. When you are able to get into that state of maturity where you find this sense of passion, then you will find that doors start to open for you, opportunities start to show up. You start to see the signs and gather more and more energy. That energy allows you to gather more and more knowledge and it becomes this kind of fluid flowing movement, not separate at all. One can move just in the direction where one is much more detached and not really working with the energy, but then one finds it unnecessarily challenging and very difficult. When you are working with the manifest reality and you are not denying it, then it is much more personal. It is very systematic, very scientific. There is an unfolding of the spirit in working with the manifest reality, a consistent, sustainable, enlightenment.

When working with the manifest naturally, it allows you to experience intimacy with the cosmic consciousness; when you are aligning yourself, then you find intimacy. The grace is always available but are you available to the grace? Spirit does not choose whether to love you or not; it is the nature of spirit to love. The manifest expression of the soul does have a choice whether to accept it or totally deny it; one does absolutely have a choice whether to deny one's own higher nature or not. Does one have a choice whether to have a higher nature or not? No. Everyone has it but one has the total freedom to be in passionate denial of it. So work with the manifest, use the Vedic science, for that is a much more natural state. There is no reason to be unnatural and in denial of anything. The manifest is the mother principle and when you deny that, you confuse yourself and then you start having issues. Working with the unfolding of spirit and living enlightenment, that is what is recommended.

It is quite natural that the mind will be scattered and will not be pointed towards consistent practice. But through the consistent practice, you start to find a natural emergence of equanimity, a natural state of integration. Practice gives rise to brilliance. You will still find resistance to the practice but then go out and serve. Practise and go out and act. Be active and serve, serve and then practise, and slowly you will start to cleanse the resistance, it starts to dissolve. Ego cleaning. The act of service is truly liberating when accompanied by an innocence in the doing. We have to be mindful of this. If we are not aware of it, then it becomes an ego game. The purpose of service is to cleanse you of the ego-mind, of the arrogance, of this false sense of pride. It is to be in that state of innocent humility which is so brilliant. It's so precious. It really raises the deserving power when we get into that state. Bringing that radiance into the external gives one a greater and greater ability to remain in spirit consciousness, in cosmic consciousness. Spirit within, spirit without, spirit within, spirit without.

Without proper understanding, proper awareness, proper knowledge, the practice is not fruitful. The practice is only fruitful with correct knowledge. So knowledge within the practice is superior to the practice. The practice without the proper knowledge is of a lesser value. It's just mechanical. It does not lead one to any higher state. One must have the proper knowledge not just about the practice but the direction that one is going in. One has to refine one's intellect. And meditation is superior to knowledge for if that knowledge is not being backed by a deeper silence, then it's just noise. If the being does not have access to silence, then it is just remaining of the surface level. For the meaning of the knowledge is directly proportional to the consciousness state of the receiver. The meaning resides in the ears of the listener. So if there is no silence, it's just noise. Without meditation, without silence, there are no roots.

And renunciation of action is superior to meditation. For as one goes within the silence, experiences arise in the beginning stages. But if one clings to these experiences, whether they are charming or not, then one remains limited. For one to progress, one has to relinquish the attachment to any experience that one has. One can experience it but one cannot remain attached to the result of one's action. On the spiritual path, you must surrender. Your job is to show up and do your practice innocently and consistently. And if you do not have the capacity to be a renunciate, to be detached, but only to cling to experiences and expectations then your actions are foul. A person who does not have the ability to act elegantly, consistently, brilliantly, without being able to renounce, without being able to just let go of the fruit, cannot make progress. For it is this state of letting go which gives rise to inner contentment. One must not be resistant to any outcome. The one who is not resistant to any outcome cannot be defeated. That kind of individual naturally gathers support and they will find great favour from nature.

For those who just act mechanically, practise mechanically, without learning it properly, there is no brilliance, no evolution. One does not know that one does not know so one walks around with the fake idea of knowing. That is ignorance. We can see that within the domain of religion, of science, in all spheres of human activity. We can see this secret ignorance, meaning it is secret from the person who is ignorant. So action without knowledge is of no use. One has to learn. For the one who goes into this deeper state, who gains proximity to their own spirit nature, freedom from all animosity and malice is born in them; there is a natural flowering of compassion. An innocent friendly nature starts to arise, a compassionate nature. If compassion is not birthing in you, then you are not progressing. As we go into cosmic consciousness, compassion has to be born. You can see the humanity and the divinity simultaneously in all. That's what compassion is. Where you can see the emptiness and the form, the formless and the form together. Where you can see the existential bliss and the existential struggle within each and every one of us. For you to be able to forgive, you have to evolve. A forgiving nature arises in the one who is practising the technology, who is moving in the direction of cosmic consciousness. That is a quality one must cultivate, forgiveness. Forgiving yourself, forgiving others, forgiving yourself, forgiving others.

Free yourself from the ideas of ownership and doership. When you have the idea of ownership, you are stressed all the time but you don't own anything. Whatever we do, we must excel in it and bring our excellence to it but we must not take ownership of it. We have to allow that great spirit to work through us, that creative intelligence to flow through us. This is your consciousness. The one who is free from the ideas of ownership and doership, who discovers this inner contentment, inner bliss, remains creative in the relative field. That inner state gives you the capacity to be equanimous with the ever-changing relative reality, to face it with a deep courage and an open heart. The one who is working on refining their energy, mastering their body and their senses, is closer to the state of cosmic consciousness. Through refining the energy, mastering the mind and the senses, one can cultivate surrender, for surrender only arises when there is a certain mastery. Only the strong can surrender. That surrender which is born out of absolute helplessness is not going to help you. The surrender that is going to uplift you is not this passive surrender. That is just inertia. The surrender that liberates you is that which is born through your dynamism, your growth.

When one does not bother the world and is not bothered by the world, one can go out and play the role fully. One can honour this reality, honour the preciousness of the play, honour the fragile nature of it all. One can see that everybody here is trying to do their best. Not bothered does not mean that you don't care. You care deeply but you're not bothered by the play of life; you care passionately but life does not destroy you, it does not

On Realising Love and Gaining Connection

overpower you. For if it overpowers you, how can you change it? To be a changemaker in the world, you have to be stronger and no longer easily distracted. You must have a certain level of mastery over your attention. The one who is rising above the duality of right and wrong, this polarizing nature of the lower mind, this craving and aversion, is close to cosmic consciousness. That is the one who is able to have presence and a certain level of lovingness for anyone they encounter. For all love is moving in the direction of Self. It blossoms as the rose, it shows up in the bird song and in the one who is able to meet friends and strangers with a loving awareness. One has to have a self-referral awareness, then one becomes free from flattery and insult, no longer engulfed by the opinions of others. The one who is filled with devotion has a loving heart and sees spirit in all things.

Lesson 13

On the Distinction between the Knower and the Known

One witnesses one's body as an object within the field of one's awareness, meaning it is an experience within that field. Sensations, feelings, even memory are a construction within the field of consciousness that we know. So the knowing aspect of Self, the knowing quality of consciousness at the subtlest level, is the quality of the soul, the quality of pure awareness. The body is known, the thoughts, memory, feelings, sensations are all known, and they are also not known. They come into the field of awareness and they dissolve from the field of awareness. What remains consistent is the witnesser of the field; what constantly modifies itself is the field. The seer remains consistent and the field keeps changing; the awareness is there but the object of awareness keeps changing. That is why one can identify oneself as oneself even though nothing in one's body stays the same forever. Nothing of one's five-year-old self is there when one is twenty-five or forty-five but we still see ourself as ourself.

The field is that which is known; the knower is that which is being known within the field. One is aware of the body, hence one says, 'my body'. We are establishing a relationship with an object based on ourself but that body is part of the field. It is arising from the field; it is a modification of the field. The knower of this body is the awareness, the one who sees the field, the ultimate witness. The ultimate subject within the knower is awareness. All desire, aversion, pleasure, pain, all values which are perceived are modifications of the field. In the cosmic scheme, the field is an expression of spirit and the knower of the field is an expression of spirit. That which is known is a modification of consciousness and the process through which it knows is consciousness. So if you are the mind, how can you master the mind? The mastery of the mind can only occur because the intellect can be refined. The ego identity only exists on the level of thought so for you to have an isolated sense of identity of who you are, you have to be aware of it. That is why you think I am this and I am that but the I is subtler than the definition.

One creates this story but the I is subtler than that; the story can change, depending on how one feels. People change their stories all the time, their whole narrative changes, but the I still remains because the I is subtler. The one who knows the field, the one who witnesses the field, the awareness, is subtler than that. But when the awareness remains denser, entangled at the surface level, then it is bound by the ego. That is why in meditation we access just the pure field of awareness; we want to experience contentless awareness. We can refine ourselves, refine our awareness, and we can begin to refine the witness. If one is witnessing only at the level of mind-body and one gets identified with it, that identification creates a state of forgetfulness and one remains in the fluctuating value of self. For the field is ever-changing, constantly fluctuating; it is dancing with intensity. If the awareness has not been stabilised and is only identified with the field, then it remains unstable, the soul remains unstable. For the nature of the field is to constantly change. This can be a cause of celebration and liberation and evolution but it can only be that when the soul starts to be aware of itself without the content. The knower begins to know itself beyond the field. Drawing the awareness to the source, the subject becomes the object, the knower becomes the known.

The Absolute simultaneously expresses as the knower and the known. It is the interaction of this within the field of spirit which gives rise to life as we know it. The natural intelligence which is organising everything, Mother Nature, is the awareness that interacts with all this ever-changing reality, the field of spirit, of diversity. All that is known is all that you see and perceive and interact with, the unified field, including the body, the mind, the perception, the senses, all of it. This dimension is of birth-sustenance-decay, birth-sustenance-decay. The whole field is conscious but the degrees of awareness differ within the distinct expressions. The awareness at the level of human, the soul, is, at its subtlest level, the ultimate witness within your own journey. You are witnessing every aspect of your being and the nature of that awareness is formless. All matter arises from consciousness; the knower and the known are all expressions of consciousness, all expressions of spirit. Consciousness is not generated by matter.

On the Distinction between the Knower and the Known   **169**

Behind these eyes is the awareness witnessing; spirit in its cosmic nature is behind all the eyes. At its deepest value, awareness is unchanging but the content of awareness is changing. The awareness is consistent but what it is aware of is evolving. This ever-changing content can move in a progressive direction or a regressive one. When it moves in the direction of elegance, there is progression. When you are miserable or unhappy, the content of your awareness is misery and unhappiness.

The soul within space-time evolves and can learn. As it develops within the interactive reality, that witnessing consciousness naturally becomes able to remain as the witness and generate a certain capacity for one to navigate one's awareness in the direction of progressive alignment. Before that can happen though, one has to learn the distinction between the knower and the known. To understand and really make sense of it, we have to realise that there is the field and then there is the knower of the field, that you are that field of silence, independent of phenomena, the witness. You are not the field; you are the knower of the field. If you take a clay pot and make five holes in it and you place a light inside, then the light shines out through the holes. So too, the senses project out awareness in that way. They interact with the relative field of reality, creating a certain flavour, a certain texture to life. To experience the flower, one has to know the flower; without the knower, there can be no knowing of the flower. So the knower is not a passive knower, the knower is active, is the one who knows of the possibility of the flower. The knower and the known are united in that. The known is only known within the awareness field of the knower. So that which is known modifies itself; it shows up differently depending on who is the knower. When the bee interacts with the flower, the quality of the flower is very distinct from the quality which is known by a human when they interact with it. So the knowing alters because it is dependent on the knower but there is this collaboration between the two values of the manifest. The knower and the known give rise to this world of diversity.

The awareness is not just within the human; it is within all the different species. It is not just the human consciousness which collapses the field into this perceivable reality. The field itself is consciousness and within that field are the two values of the ever-changing and the knowing. They are part of that same whole. It is the nature of the field. It is inherent within the manifest reality. The awareness of the ever-changing dance and the dance are eternal; the witness to the dance and the dance are eternal. When you are interacting, you feel consistently validated; your point of view of reality is consistently validated but to think that one's version of reality is the only version is deluded. There is a version of reality that an ant is witnessing and a butterfly is witnessing and a bee is witnessing and a bird is witnessing which are all very distinct from what we are witnessing but when they are witnessing, they are doing so exactly in the same manner as you or I. The knower is what gives flavour to the known which pervades the entire reality, unmoving and also moving. So as the bird moves, the awareness of the bird moves with it. As the human moves, the awareness of the human moves with it. The field can keep modifying based on the knower.

We witness the spirit within and the spirit without as the manifest, the knower of the field and the field. Indivisible like space but also rising as modifications seemingly divided, yet fundamentally remaining undivided. All creation is known within it, all that maintains is known within it, all destruction is known within it, bringing forth the ever-changing and creating the joys and sorrows within itself. The experience is of duality for there is the knower and the object of knowledge. But both are ultimately expressions of that singularity which maintains its indivisible nature, hence it's all-pervading. It is localisation which gives rise to the experience of duality in that field. So the field will keep changing and keep evolving and dancing. It is not the cause of suffering. It is the knower's relationship to the known, dependent on whatever lens one is looking through, that creates suffering. When one understands this, one is liberated from suffering.

The value of consciousness is the soul, expressing as this mind-body complex. But awareness is present at all levels and transcendent simultaneously, so as you are experiencing body awareness, you are also experiencing spatial awareness and sensory awareness. You are aware of the sensory input that is coming into your system; there is energetic awareness. As you breathe in and you breathe out, you see there is a subtle movement in your energy. There is awareness at the level of thought, of feeling; understanding is occurring. There is awareness at all these levels. And at the fundamental level of being, there is the experience of 'my' body even though one understands one is not the body. So it is important for us to understand this distinction between the knower and that which is known and to realise the knower and the known share an intricate relationship. The knower is not a passive knower; the knower is an active knower and there is communication in both directions. The field is reaching into the knower and the knower is reaching into the known for they are modifications of that one spirit.

So meditation is supporting knowledge, knowledge is supporting meditation. The practice is supported by knowledge, knowledge is refined by meditation. As the knower refines, what is known is refined. One naturally becomes humble, loses arrogance, gains innocence and a deep sense of fulfilment starts to arise. A sense of security starts to arise and insecurity naturally melts away. This constant effort to build a personality and find validation from the external environment ceases. This is something to cultivate because the ego-mind is constantly obsessed with itself, moving in circles around itself, ungrounded and without stability. When awareness is not available, arrogance is the natural tendency. When the light of wisdom arises, one transcends this pretentious, hypocritical, diabolical nature. As the light of awareness starts to shine, one becomes authentic, clear, humble. In the denser state, when one is constantly in conflict with oneself, with the relative field of reality, it is 'me' against the Universe, 'me' against myself.

As this light of knowledge starts to gain strength, the awareness starts to be enlivened, then there is greater adaptability. One is then more accommodating to others, more inclusive, for the true leader knows how to adapt and accommodate.

As long as one is bound by the ego, one has this false sense of self. The soul is totally oblivious of its own soul nature and is bound by this image that is generated by the intellect, based on the incorrect memories accumulated through its interaction with the space-time continuum. This idea of ownership, this idea of me and mine, leads to suffering. So as the wisdom is shining within you, naturally this non-ownership, this non-identification, arises and the ability to care without projection or attachment grows. One is able to care without holding it against the person that one is caring for. If caring for someone is accompanied with the idea of, "Look how much I am doing for you," then you are setting yourself up for trouble. Service without attachment, without projection, is the quality which we must be aware of cultivating within ourselves. This and equanimity which comes from the ability to be at home within oneself. Equanimity only belongs to those who are able to be at home within themselves and find refuge in their own Buddha nature; those who are able to retreat not only to a physical place of seclusion but also within themselves.

It is an essential part of one's progress to be able to be in seclusion and not just engaging with the external and being constantly busy, to take time to retreat within oneself and elevate. We must cultivate this contemplative nature, the ability to enjoy one's own company and not be constantly trying to escape oneself through other people and activity. The ability to be deeply contemplative is very beneficial. It is not a passive isolation but an active, creative space, to be with oneself and to explore. To deepen one's spiritual knowledge needs consistent practice and learning. To awaken to a deeper level, there needs to be constancy in learning and learning about oneself, learning within oneself and learning through being a student. As one keeps learning, one's ability is constantly expanding. For if one is constantly learning and evolving, then one is able to really dance with life. When any qualities which are opposing this are cultivated, they lead one to ignorance. But through the light of knowledge, this can be changed. What you put out, so you get back. What you put out into the field, the field responds to. You put friendliness out into the field, the field gives back friendliness.

Lesson 14

On the Three Vibrational States of the Leela

The one who has mastered the mind, who has a deep, inner contemplative presence, an inner silence, is somebody who has access to that deep field of silence. The greater the silence in you, the greater the wisdom. Without silence, there is no wisdom. All wisdom lives in the house of silence and this supreme wisdom is liberating. Liberation is not at the end of life; it is not outside of life. It's important to understand this. The whole point of our existence is not to get out of existing in this manifest expression. Liberation is a particular skill in living; it's a state of being while available here and now. The nature of the Self is timeless, eternal, there is no other place to go to. Liberation is a state to be realised within oneself through awareness, through supreme knowledge. For what one knows, one becomes. The wise one realises their liberation.

The idea of liberation is often thought of as only achievable at the end of life but if there is only eternity, what is the end? If your nature is timeless, then there is no end to you; beginningless and endless. So liberation can't be the end. It is the gaining of knowingness, the awakening to that degree of consciousness where you begin to exist in an elegant manner. One is not imprisoned by life, this is not a prison; liberation is not freedom from the field, the field is magnificent. The prison is ignorance so through supreme knowledge liberation is realised within. Those who gain wisdom, who begin to embody this knowledge, gain freedom from time. The one who is awake, who is aligned with the dreamer and not with the dream, is not afraid when the dream finishes and restarts. This is a field of love and it is only through love that the infinite, the spirit, modifies into different stages of evolution, different layers of reality. This is a creative act, born out of supreme love, that constant presence that permeates the entire existence. Knowledge is love and love is knowledge. Without knowingness, there is no love; love without knowledge, without wisdom, is an emotion, fragile and fickle.

So this liberation is not escaping for there is nowhere to escape to. It is to realise one's true Self and for that, learning is required. When spirit is realising, then the localised value gains freedom, for the nature of spirit is freedom. There is no more fear of anything, no burden of existence in this dimension or other dimensions. The nature of spirit is to exist so that we can exist and so to be in existence is divine, is sacred. This cycle is created within the womb of life, the multi-dimensional nature of reality. Within this manifest reality, we are bound by the laws of trinity. The aspects of this are the three vibrational states within the field. They give the structural value within nature, the dynamic value within nature and the intelligent value within nature. So there is structure, dynamism and intelligence within the field and the observer of the field. Now within the level of the mind, these three take on a different value. Structure becomes ignorance, inert and heavy. Dynamism becomes activity driven by desire and fear. Intelligence becomes a state of illumination, supreme wisdom and joy.

So within the individual, the finite being, the inert, actionless one is attached to that inaction. The active one becomes caught up in cause and effect, being busy, always trying to get somewhere, to manage life, then dying and being born still running around in the ever-repeating known, lifetimes upon lifetimes, desire filled and replaced by more desire. The intelligence is the state of illuminated joy, pure wisdom. All this is inherent within nature and to be transcended first using action to get out of inertia, then intelligence to get out of action and then intelligence to get out of overthinking. This transcendence of these states and then coming back into their realm, transcending and returning, increases the value of joy and pure wisdom within us because it is illuminating, immaculate and flawless. It is the vibration of bliss and knowledge. At the denser level, the action is born out of desire and then there is attachment to the fruit of that desire. It repeats, desire, action, fruit of the desire, attachment to the fruit of the desire. But the desire changes. When one's state of mind changes, then there is revolution at the level of cause. When the consciousness state starts to change and rises to the level of illuminated joy and pure wisdom, then the desire changes and so the action changes. That action changes the fruit. When the consciousness state changes, one is no longer attached to the fruit and so the fruit is more fulfilling and fulfilment generates fulfilment.

One is drawn to joy and wisdom or to action or to ignorance. Within the ignorance, the driving force is self-destruction. Within the action, the driving force is desire, even though that desire will ultimately lead to frustration and destruction that is not obvious to the individual. In the ignorance though, one knows that what one is doing is destructive but one is helpless to stop it. So action can slide into ignorance. At any given time within one individual, either ignorance, action or supreme joy can be dominating. One is dominating and another is subordinate. The moment one ceases to be busy, one goes into a self-destructive pattern and before you know it, you are in a vicious trap. Active people might be always achieving things, doing a lot, but they find no bliss in it, no radiance is there. They don't have the capacity to be still; the moment they are still they go into the inert, ignorant state. There is a fear of not doing, so they always fill up the silence with all kinds of stuff, plans are made, every minute is controlled. When this starts to become refined, both the dynamism and stillness start to become refined, they merge together into pure wisdom and illuminated joy.

In illuminated joy, dynamism is there and so too is stillness, together in perfect harmony. The individual can be active in a relevant manner but also find stillness. Stillness does not dominate, activity does not dominate, both exist in harmony. There is stillness in dynamism and dynamism in stillness. For that to happen, there has to be a revolution. To create illuminated joy, there has to be a conscious effort to move in the direction of it, the direction of supreme wisdom. One has to expose one's awareness to those values, meaning, moving towards wisdom, illumination, spirit. One has to start to question one's behaviour. One has to start to change one's daily life; what one consumes, what one is giving time to, one has to start to shift one's worldview. As illuminated joy starts to increase, discernment increases, the intellect is refined and self-regulation is naturally born. One finds less and less resistance and spontaneous right action starts to become more available to one. There is a greater peace, a greater silence within oneself, a greater wisdom and joy start to become available when tuning into the vibrational frequency of supreme wisdom.

Within the spectrum of that supreme wisdom are many beings, beings who are very elevated and also just good people, happy people, kinder, less self-righteous people. In the hunger of the ever-active mind is this feeling of never being enough, never having enough, always finding problems, a restlessness. The activity which arises from supreme wisdom is stillness. One is no longer bound by craving and aversion, craving and aversion, the hole which cannot be filled. But in the relative field of reality, there will always be duality. Wherever there is light, there will be shadow. This vibrational frequency in nature which creates structure has a density in individuals because we are part of nature, but one can also get stuck in it, the mind becomes rigid. And the ever-active mind can be stuck too, in that endless loop of busy, busy, busy, chasing, chasing, chasing, being the hamster on the wheel forever.

So one needs to tune into the vibrational frequency of the supreme wisdom.

These are all inherent properties; they are not flaws in the soul. They are vibrational frequencies, certain modes of behaviour, modes of thinking, modes of being and they can easily be altered. One must learn to self-observe and see where one needs correction but that correction can only arise from a place of non-judgemental awareness. If it is a critic-based awareness, then naturally wherever there is judgement, there is going to be a defence and one can find oneself stuck in the loop of critiquing and defending, critiquing and defending, critiquing and defending. So when we realise that they are inherent within the manifest reality, we don't have to get identified with the modes of behaviour or thinking. We can work with our energy and shift the frequency, move in the direction of refinement where ignorance becomes stillness, action becomes clear and dynamic and they both merge and harmonize in supreme wisdom, evolutionary action moving toward brilliance.

As the intellect becomes refined, the being starts to experience inner illumination and a lightness of being. When it is being maintained consistently, it starts to be the predominant mode of being, of behaviour, of thinking; it becomes the predominant vibration within the individual and so naturally creates an upward, evolutionary movement. Even when the body drops, the individual experiences luminosity and finds themself in dimensions which correspond to that luminous consciousness state, that awareness filled with wisdom. For the dropping of the body is just another shift in the level of the field. The field changes, the awareness continues. When the death of the body happens, the one who has been living in greater alignment with the value of that supreme wisdom experiences the celestial realms. For it's all happening within the consciousness field; body changes and the field modifies, the field is in alignment with the consciousness state that the individual is maintaining most consistently. Where the individual finds themself depends on their consciousness state. So the supreme wisdom not only lifts up the value of life here, it also lifts up the value of life beyond here. When you are living well, then death brings no fear. For after death, you will find yourself just within your own awareness. As in life, so in death.

Love is still available when you are in the state of ignorance or action too; there is no judgement complaining. There is brilliance in all levels, in all species. Life is sacred in all directions. There is brilliance in all directions; human beings don't have the copyright to the peak of evolution. There is choice but one has to decide, one can move from one vibrational state to another or one can remain stuck for lifetimes. The reward of supreme wisdom is pure joy. The reward of persistent activity is struggle. The reward of inert ignorance is increasing ignorance. The beauty of it is though, it doesn't matter because there is only one consciousness so when anyone is awakening, it sends out ripples. Anyone acting from a place of supreme wisdom, a place of compassion, kindness, humility, generosity, gratefulness, is sending ripples out into the field of Self. Wisdom flows or aggression flows or confusion flows. People who are in a confused state don't know how to think; they let others do the thinking for them which creates fear. One of the great tools for mass brainwashing is to create fear and divisiveness. The active mind can much more easily control the confused mind. But those who are evolving naturally increase in the value of supreme wisdom, they break out of the ever-repeating known and move upward, toward brilliance, wisdom, supreme knowledge and that then informs the action, creating action which is clear, an intellect which is clear, a heart which is engaged and connected.

Through the practice of meditation, diving deep into that pure being beyond the vibrational states, one begins to realise that it is not 'me' who is ignorant or ceaselessly active. It is occurring in that vibrational frequency. Understanding this allows one to evolve very easily. The problem is that we identify with our structures of thinking and so we think that is who we are. But any identity which is making you so angry is made up from borrowed ideas. It is just a product of conditioning, of structures of thought. These vibrations are all part of the manifest reality; cognizing this allows one to become detached from it. That detachment moves one in the direction of evolutionary living. Through our meditation, we can see that these tendencies, our ideas, the way we think and behave, are all part of our conditioning. They are not who we are. These are just patterns within nature and they serve their purpose. Every frequency serves a purpose; they are not mistakes.

Lesson 15
On Climbing the Tree of Life

All this wisdom is an invitation to wake up to a deeper knowing in the now, which can create a revolution within our own being; it can totally transform the way we see, perceive and engage with life within and without. Now. It's a reminder not to get lost in the linear line of time, to remain at that level of the industrialized brain which is just trying to get somewhere else, procrastinating transformation. This does not result in evolution. The line of time does not necessarily mean the progression of the individual. Of course, in time, a greater integration and realisation can occur. Time can keep serving as a tool.

The tree of life is used as a metaphor for creation. Within that great cosmic tree, time flows but the tree remains here. Within our relative experience, when we meet the tree, life, it is always now, it never goes anywhere, it is not on its way to any place. The passing of time in the tree shows the aging of the tree, but the tree is always here with its roots planted deep in the soil. You can see over the years that time is flowing through the tree. With that flow of time, there are changes occurring within but the tree remains here. For there to be the cognition of the flow of time, there has to be the tree. In the context of the tree, the flow of time is shown in the changes that you witness in the tree. For you to understand the flow of time, for you to experience the flow of time, you require a certain object which is undergoing change. It is the experience of this change in the object of your awareness that gives you the experience of time moving. In the absence of any object in the field of your awareness, you cannot experience time.

The tree will live a long time but there is a value of now to it because the tree will eventually no longer be locatable here. The manifest reality within that cosmic timeline also comes in and out of existence, it is maintaining its beginningless-ness. The fundamental spirit remains eternal but all the content, the localised values, go through the cycles of time. For the nature of spirit is time. Time is within it, so the spirit remains and everything that modifies within space-time comes in and out of existence. All time is now. You measure change in the now, that is how you experience the passage of time. The passage of time is experienced by the observer because there is a memory and when there is a change from that memory, a difference between this now and that memory of a previous now, that gives the psychological experience of time. One experiences it all in a linear progression. But it is all experienced in the tree of creation, which is always here in the now.

There are two distinct meanings: the tree of life has its roots in a superior dimension and the branches flow downwards but on the level of the body the roots are in the brain; the spinal column with the cerebral spinal fluid and the nerve complex are the branches and the leaves. So within the body, the tree is upside down and through the yogic techniques, we draw the energy up to the root, feeding the root because if we don't nourish the root, it can't thrive. You need to nourish the root if you want the tree to be healthy. When we draw the energy up through the spine, it rises up and feeds the brain. At the higher state, this tree of creation is fed from its roots in a subtler dimension of consciousness. On the level of consciousness, on the level of the unmanifest, the roots are at the subtlest level of being and the trunk with the colourless sap is the spirit; that same colourless sap then expresses in the branches and as the leaf, meaning knowledge.

The good health of a tree has to start with the nourishment of the root. If the tree is healthy, the branches are strong and the leaves are plentiful. But no matter how much you feed the root, if you keep cutting the branches back, then the growth of the tree is stunted. For it is through the leaf that the root is nourished. Without the leaf, the tree cannot grow and thrive. It cannot provide shade or shelter to the birds. It cannot produce fruits or impact positively on the environment. It cannot serve. The value of the tree is expressed through the leaves and when they fall, they then nourish the soil. In the tree of life, the leaf is the knowledge, that field of knowledge. As spirit starts to move as the tree, the infinite branches expand and are interconnected. On the level of the individual, the roots branch out moving in both directions, upward and downward, meaning we move in both evolutionary or regressive directions. The root, the brain, can create progression or regression; the energy can flow either way. The energy does not discriminate whether you grow plants with thorns or plants which sting or fruit trees, the water will nourish them all. It does not judge or choose. When energy is not drawn up, it has the potential to spiral downward.

The tree of life continues on a cosmic scale and also on the human scale. In the cosmic scheme, the branches going up and down mean the tree is not just here in the realm of the manifest earth; it is also in astral realms for as the branches spread, the tree develops roots in different regions. Within our own body, the branches of the tree are that flow of energy moving outward. Wherever we interact consistently, we start developing more roots there. Those roots create more growth, more branches and leaves. So if your energy is consistently moving in a regressive direction, then you will start to establish roots there. Once those roots are established, they become part of you and make deep imprints on your psyche. Then certain tendencies that get implanted start to have their own lifecycle over which you cease to have control. Like when a young person smokes a cigarette to look cool but before long the habit has taken root and they have to smoke. They struggle if they want to stop; they have no control over the desire anymore. So a person wants to be grateful but can't be. Every day they say they're going to be grateful but by the evening they're ungrateful again because the branches go out in all directions and wherever the branches grow, they establish roots there. When the energy is imbalanced, we have to find support; all our energy then goes to support the imbalance of our own nature. We work tirelessly every day to remain imbalanced; all our activities are in service of maintaining the imbalance. Cosmically, as the universe is within, so the universe is without.

The tree of life, the creation, is bewildering because of its infinite nature, because one cannot see the beginning of it, the root. Because of its infinite nature, many of us live on the peripheral level of reality, remaining only on the surface, overwhelmed by the enormity of the tree, unable to discover the main root. But the wise one goes to the root, nourishes the root, for the roots are nourished by whichever way the branches are going. By rising up in the world, by transcending, we can serve the world. We draw the energy through our meditation, simultaneously transcending and nourishing. Through transcendence, we nourish the tree in the manifest reality. But if one just remains on the surface value, then one does not know the nature of the tree. One is lost, one does not realise the interconnectedness of it all.

By transcending, by going to that primordial being, one is able to rise beyond the tree of creation. When we go deep into the third eye, deep into the root, all time disappears. One finds that one transcends the relative phenomena, the relativity of this tree. By going to the root, you transcend. When one doesn't practise, one remains oblivious, entangled in pseudo-roots and never finding enough vitality. When the roots are not being fed, the leaves will become unhealthy, knowledge will not be there. If one does not have the ability to go to the root of the tree, then the knowledge one accumulates becomes irrelevant as times change. Adaptability to the changing times is required for healthy growth for if it is true wisdom, then it will adapt. On the healthy tree, leaves go through their cycle and new leaves keep growing and shedding. That's the flow of wisdom. If it is just accessed on the level of the leaf, then it is information. The one who is able to have complete access to wisdom within the relative manifest, within the perishable and imperishable, formless and form, all dimensions not just in one, is an integrated being. That is the nature of the enlightened, integrated being.

Focus on evolution, moving towards becoming free; transcending the tree while being aware of the tree. Within the yogic theology, the seat of the sun and the moon is the third eye, the two-petaled lotus, but it is not the sun and the moon of the external reality which illuminates; it is the inner light. As the energy rises up to that level of being, as one starts to transcend, that energy, the fire which was going downwards in our regressive behaviour, starts to rise up. Then the sun, the moon, the fire, all the light merges into the light of Self for ultimately there is only one light, the light of spirit. This causeless light isn't just a metaphor; the whole universe is filled with light. The entire intergalactic space is filled with light; there is light everywhere. This is the sensory universe and then there is a universe beyond the senses which is experienced independent of sensory perception. Both universes are relevant for both are within consciousness; one is experienced through the agency of the senses and the other is independent of them. As the energy rises up, then the light of the sun, the moon and the fire merge to become the golden current; so one does not need the external light to be illuminated. This is the light of Self, the light of spirit. That primordial state is self-illuminated, that light which illuminates the entire intergalactic universe and the Self, accessible at the root level. The individualised value, the soul, is but a fragment of the whole. We are totality but totality is not just us as we know ourself. It is all else.

Life is to be celebrated and one cannot celebrate without simultaneously liberating, for without liberation there is no celebration. Joy and freedom go hand in hand, wisdom and love go hand in hand. So the soul, expressing through the senses, enjoys the show and rejoices in this play. You are a soul expressing as this body. The body is an expression of you, the soul, and is in awe of this manifest reality. It is truly miraculous. But it is only those who are endowed with the eyes of wisdom who are able to see the soul. Otherwise, the knower remains unknown to the knower; the ignorant do not know the soul. When it is identified with ignorance, the soul does not know the soul, the Atman does not know itself for seeing is not believing, seeing is seeing. A lot of people believe they are souls, but they do not act like it. Believing you are a soul is different from knowing you are a soul. The ignorant do not know, do not see the soul while it is the body and even when it ceases to be the body. Only the wise who have that capacity, observe it. Only those who have the eyes of wisdom learn to see and when they see themselves as the soul, as consciousness, then the way they show up is very different. Belief is only a quality of those who do not know, it is contrary to knowing. Knowing is an antidote to believing. When you know, you don't need to believe.

The ignorant do not know. The wise do. Knowing changes you, alters you, transforms the way you live this life, the way you show up.

The soul has to be known, has to self-realise. Those who are able to raise their energy, who have a specific methodology, can realise themselves. Just having the intention is not enough. Intention is a wonderful and important part but those who are not working with the subtler aspects, not purifying their hearts, cleansing their energy, their minds, not transcending the clutches of conditioning, will not be able to realise their true Self. One has to raise one's energy, purify at the heart and maintain the practice, otherwise one's intentions are futile. They are lost. When that energy rises and it stays at the heart, then everything is functioning at its full potential and is fully supported.

These teachings need to be valued; to understand them, embody them and realise them is to understand the purpose in life. But the purpose of life cannot be discovered without the inner awakening. Until one is awakened, the purpose is a projection of the ego-mind. Without the genuine exploration of self and the evolution of self, there is only the never-ending insanity. But once you realise yourself, once you awaken, then you are supremely powerful while being simultaneously aware of the impermanent, fleeting nature of it all. You can only discover meaning when you truly realise the absolute meaninglessness of it all. You must first face the absolute absurdity of it all, the ideas and structures created by human thought, without reacting to it; just face it with a deep open heart. Then you can discover the meaning. You cannot discover meaning without meaninglessness; you cannot find light without being in the darkness. There can be no timelessness without there being time.

Lesson 16
On Cultivating Qualities of Conscious Growth

The journey into wisdom has to have an integrated approach. We have to realise that wisdom is not merely a bunch of sentences or a song celestial. When we approach the teachings from an integrated place, we look at them as a journey, an exploration, not something to rush through just to reach a conclusion. They are an opportunity to really come to a deeper state of realisation. Human beings are prone to misunderstandings; it is just part of who we are. We consistently misunderstand, but often we confuse that misunderstanding with understanding. The non-continuous self is the ego-mind, that personality haphazardly put together, this sense of identity that one has created, and it does not continue. The conscious awareness continues because it is timeless. Misunderstanding happens when we confuse the non-continuous, egoic self with the actual Self. If you do not have the deeper understanding, you just meet the teachings at a particular level and use them to fit in with your own preconceived idea, instead of exploring them. The ego doesn't exist, the soul does; that awareness within which the ego is constructed exists. Ego is just a hallucination, a shadow. Wisdom should be like a song, to be continually explored not from a place of confusion but from a place of deep, inner inquiry.

Without a foundation in maturity, the soul is caught up in the storm. Then we become fragile and find life more challenging than it needs to be. Without building that strong foundation of wisdom, nourishing the root of our tree, we cannot discover the meaning in life. There are many qualities that naturally emerge from a being who is rising in the direction of pure joy, supreme wisdom and gaining inner illumination, qualities that one must build on and make a part of how one shows up. Compassion, generosity and stability are eternally valuable, relevant irrespective of the location or timeline. The fire has the quality of warmth whether the fire was lit three thousand years ago or three thousand years from now. These are essential qualities, they are independent of time, independent of situation, independent of circumstance. These qualities are not beliefs. They are the natural qualities of a being who is gaining that inner illumination, qualities that naturally radiate from that state of higher consciousness. They are to be cultivated within ourself and one must be alert, bringing them into the forefront of one's consciousness by giving them attention. These are dynamic states to be lived, expressed and practised. They are not dead, inert structures of thought. We cannot take just a part of these teachings in isolation; one must have a complete, comprehensive understanding. One can misunderstand the teachings when one takes them in isolation. To gain an integrated vision of life, one needs a dynamic cultivation of these aspects which will create a stable character in the relative field of reality. Like the fire which is naturally hot, so it is natural for the being who is rising in a higher state of consciousness to be wise, compassionate and have insight, stability and staying power.

These qualities start with fearlessness and the path to fearlessness begins with acknowledging that there is fear. One cannot be fearless without acknowledging that one is afraid for unacknowledged fear wreaks havoc. One of the fundamental qualities of being identified with the ego state is fear. It arises from the misunderstanding of Self, mis-identification of Self. When the Self is attached to the ego-mind, it experiences the state of disconnect, isolation, a sense of constantly being overwhelmed; thinking is dominated by fear and, as I've said, fear is one of the greatest tools used to control and manipulate. But for you to be manipulated, you have to agree to it; without your agreement no one can manipulate you. So fear is there and one must acknowledge it. There is no glory in denying the presence of fear. First accept it, then transcend it. You can only transcend that which you first acknowledge. To cross the river, you must first acknowledge the river is there. The denial of fear is not courage. It is the acknowledgement that there is fear that then drives behaviour that allows one to transcend it. The whole integrated approach allows us to be in that state of fearlessness. Cognition of our own true nature, embodying the teachings in our life, allows fearlessness to be the natural outcome. Being fearful is a part of being human, a natural part of reality. Without awareness there can be no fearlessness. As this light of wisdom dawns in us, then fear has to drop. If we find it still arising, it just means we have to correct our understanding, go deeper within ourself. The nature of the evolved consciousness state is fearlessness. Acknowledge it and transcend it while simultaneously shining the light of wisdom from within. The acknowledgement that there is fear is already the sign of greatness. It's the beginning of becoming fearless. One cannot just be fearless by deciding it; one has to be aware and then practise transcendence of it, for fear is a very base emotion.

As one aligns with the vibrational state of supreme wisdom and true joy, as we go deeper into our meditation from a place of compassion and devotion, there is natural purification of the heart. Energy moving in the direction of the heart is cultivating heart intelligence. The quality of a being who is in that state will have a strong electromagnetic field for the heart is the organ which generates the strongest electromagnetic field. The electromagnetic field of the heart is not rigid, it is dynamic and when you are in that state it becomes enormous. As you radiate from that place, from the heart, you can affect the people in that space. Aligning ourself with that vibrational state of supreme wisdom naturally enlivens the heart.

One must learn to be steadfast in the integrated wisdom, not in the opinions, the isolated points of view, the ideologies but the wisdom of these teachings. It is integrated wisdom that is dynamic and steadfast. This deep commitment to the wisdom is a quality we cultivate that is born out of our continued practice of it throughout our life. It is a commitment to gaining greater understanding, to realising that the crisis that one experiences is based on one's consciousness state and that if one can alter one's consciousness state, the crisis diminishes. It is through the light of wisdom that the crisis, the problems we perceive, dissolves. As our awareness gains a greater level of understanding than the understanding which is generating the crisis, we find our problems are resolved. The crisis does not get resolved by remaining the same. It's a steadfast commitment to maintaining wisdom, the practice of wisdom and the wisdom that is born out of the practice. As we evolve, then naturally greater wisdom is born out of that unity. The greater the unity, the greater the wisdom flows. The lesser the unity, the lesser the wisdom. They are directly proportional to each other.

One must cultivate a naturally generous nature. This is not just about giving funds but generosity born out of a certain consciousness state, rising from the state of unity. This also means to be generous with our love, with our attention, with ourselves, for as we gain unity, the resourcefulness within us increases. The greater the resourcefulness, the greater the ability to give and serve; what you can give is not bound to a certain resource. If you are stuck in the concept of lack, then it is difficult to be generous. Remember, whatever you put out into the field returns back; that's the law of nature. So a natural generosity of being starts to rise and this generosity is a state of love, connection, attention, wisdom and sincerity. You have infinite resources; everybody has something to offer irrespective of the accumulation of stuff. This is not generosity based on material wealth.

One must learn mastery of the senses, of our attention. It is both a practice and a state. We spend our energy through our senses; we spend our lives interacting through our sensory awareness. The mastery over our senses is mastery of our attention, for our attention follows our senses and our senses follow our attention. One has to have a systematic integrated approach to achieve this, not just an intention to do so. Knowledge and action are not separate from each other.

Renunciation, sacrificing the lower aspects and building a consistent practice, again needs to be a constant practice, a way of living one's life, acting with others, being in the world, not just giving up some aspect.

Self-study must be practised. Truly studying the self not just to show off but as a deep part of learning who we are with a genuinely awakened inner love of wisdom, of expansion, is part of the responsibility for your self-growth. Studying yourself, observing yourself, not analysing and becoming self-obsessed but self-study.

Practising the commitment to short-term challenges to build character, build up our energy, to cultivate progressive seeds within our psyche is not some punishment. It is the building up of oneself. When you take short-term challenges which are based on a certain specific evolutionary vision within yourself, dedicated to growing yourself, to develop yourself, those are edifying for all.

Being straightforward, clear, not fooling oneself but being aware of one's intention and being straightforward is when your intention and your attention are matching, are in alignment; you're not fooling anyone especially yourself. That happens when you observe yourself, become aware and align yourself. Then one stops saying one thing and meaning something else.

Nonviolence should be practised. The transcendence of violence is a powerful state of being, that deep state, responding to the need without harm is not just being a doormat. It is a powerful, brilliant state where you can learn a greater unity, fulfil the need of the hour and there is no violence in you. The absence of violence is only gained when you're moving in the direction of unity. The consciousness state which is identified with the ego can never be nonviolent. This is a state reached through conscious practice, transcending, moving in the direction of unity.

Moving in the direction of truth must be a constant practice, discovering the truth as one gains alignment, for truth has to be discovered. It is not just about speaking the truth because the speaker speaks from their consciousness state. If the consciousness state is aligned with density, how can one speak the truth? Humans think they are right, they have the right truth and the other one is lying; anyone who disagrees with their opinion is a liar. It's an absurd thing to think your opinion is the one true truth. Life includes different opinions from others and the one moving in the direction of their own divine nature naturally has access to that understanding. They are able to see the truth beneath the surface, they can understand different points of view. Their capacity to understand naturally increases, a willingness to learn, to engage in a deepening of understanding. It seems risky to the ego-mind to relinquish the attachment to one's point of view in favour of gaining a deeper understanding. It requires courage.

The transcendence of anger must be practised, that inner anger that grips you in the gut. When one transcends that place of resentment, there is an absence of resentment, it disappears. Not an absence of fire, the fierceness is a natural state of leadership. It is not some kind of flatline, wishy-washy state. It is the relinquishing of that state of resentment born out of pain as a reaction to suffering within oneself, a reaction to fear. Fear and pain give rise to anger which builds and boils within oneself and causes resentment. One consciously has to transcend this victim identity, this identity which thrives on self-righteous anger.

Learn to let go of identification, of attachment. When one discovers greater states of bliss within oneself, then one is able to naturally let this go.

One must seek inner peace, that peace found in that deep, inner silence. For silence and peace are connected. Peace cannot be known without the experience of silence. It is only in the experience of deep silence that one knows peace. That is why in a world where people have no understanding of silence, peace is hard to come by. We keep fighting in the name of peace. Peace is not a set of circumstances; it is a consciousness state. It's an experience of silence. The greater the silence within us, the greater the peace.

Learning how to use our speech to elevate, not in a destructive manner, then being aware of the power of our expression, we realise the power of creation inherent within our words.

We must cultivate a deep, consistent compassion and loving kindness. We need to have compassion for all beings, all things, without judgement.

Transcendence of the persistence of the mind to consume is to be practised in order to release our minds from the desire for more, more, more which is never enough. Then we can move towards growth rather than consumption.

Being aware of different aspects, we can realise a balanced and integrated harmonious state. For something to be true, the other doesn't have to be false. Divisive partisan thinking is not the way of the wise; the wise know the middle way. It's not a compromise; it is the elegant state, that ability to synthesize and come to a holistic understanding.

Build strong principles, have a keen commitment to one's inner guiding principles and maintain them.

Non-restlessness is the absence of restlessness within ourselves. In the presence of restlessness, one finds a futile pursuit of being ever-busy, constantly engaged in activity. One is busy just for the sake of busyness because one does not know how to be with oneself.

Cultivate the glow, the radiance. As you practise, you begin to work with your inner energy and there is a natural glow that starts to radiate as you are able to gather up your energy. That quality of engaged presence rises up and there is a natural radiance in a being who is illuminating their inner Self.

Forgiveness is essential for our own liberation. If we do not know how to forgive then we are maintaining that victim identity at a certain level. In order to transcend that victim identity, it's an essential part of one's growth. We must learn to forgive others and ourselves.

If we cultivate staying power, then we are able to stay with equanimity irrespective of the fluctuations that happen. Circumstances change but you stay. Things get difficult, things get easy, and you stay. If you don't have that staying power, then you remain on that level of fluctuation. Staying power equals deserving power.

Cultivate the art of cleansing, releasing toxicity from your system, letting go of toxic thought patterns, toxic memories, toxic substance. Learn to clear out and cleanse your system.

The absence of resentment is all part of letting go of that anger, of not actively hating, not holding on to this toxicity of hatred anymore.

Without non-arrogance, humility, there is no learning, no growth, no receptivity. Humility is not the absence of confidence; humility is born out of confidence.

These qualities are natural to those who are aligned to their true nature but not to the one who is out of tune and committed to remaining out of tune. Energy can move in either direction, toward progression or regression. So if one is moving in the direction of regression, then one is gaining negatively but when one is moving in the evolutionary direction toward higher stages of consciousness, one is gaining the celestial value. Now, within any movement, whether one way or the other, one can see there are different aspects of being. Some beings have been moving in one direction for a while and so have gained a greater ability within that value. Some have been out of tune for so long they have become attached to that state, committed to it through their ignorance, totally drawn to that frequency. But none of it is permanent; practices can change and movement in the other direction can occur. The celestial value is available within each and every one of us.

These qualities naturally emerge as we take care of our consciousness state and get more in tune with our essential nature. We stabilise our own consciousness when we start to build a strong foundation and then we thrive. Our own sacred nature is there for us all but we have to claim it and realise it. If illumination is thrust upon us, then it is not illumination, for what you gain through your own practice, through your own action, has a sweetness to it and keeps the relative game interesting. When it is just handed to you, then it doesn't have the sweetness. By gaining greater and greater alignment with that sacred value, attuning ourselves to wisdom and expanding our consciousness, we are able to effortlessly embody these qualities. There is a lot of energy wasted on the manipulation of opinion. When the ego feels it is not worthy, it spends time just posturing, looking for validation. One lies to oneself and creates all kinds of masks to wear just to be liked, to manipulate the opinion of others so one can feel a slight worthiness. This is not a desirable quality. It does not generate bliss and it keeps us ungrounded.

The greater this undesirable state is, the greater the arrogance. The wise can only be wise when they are willing to learn and that requires being radically open to the possibility of not being right, open to the possibility that you have something to learn, and that requires humility, openness, receptivity. Arrogance is a state of shutting down, closing the doors to the light of wisdom. So those who align with the lower tendencies, the need to stay busy and remain in ignorance, are out of tune. But those who consciously align themselves are in tune. Then you don't need to be afraid. Ignorance does not know action or inaction; the ignorant one is constantly bewildered, acts when they shouldn't act, doesn't act when they should, tries to change what they can't, accepts what can be changed. Confusion is there and one feels helpless. To know the difference, one has to develop intuition, insight, develop that silence within, then one knows when to act, when to create change. When we attune ourselves to our own lower tendencies, the self is the loser and gets into a destructive state. One must be mindful of these tendencies because even though one is born with divine nature, one must align oneself to it, to the teachings, grow and evolve. We must establish ourself, build a strong foundation within ourself and evolve while always being aware to not give up our power to our lower tendencies. In the relative field of reality, duality will be there because it is all part of the play.

Lesson 17
On Moving from Faith to Knowing

These teachings are multi-layered and the meaning remains hidden if they are not decoded. If one does not fully understand them but has a certain level of belief, they have faith; all beings have faith in something, some idea, even the one who has no faith has faith in no faith. Whatever one's conscious state is, one's belief is born out of that. It conforms to the level of one's evolution. What we believe in, we become. So it is not about faith or no faith. It is about moving in the direction of knowing or just remaining on the level of believing because whatever you believe in you become and your activities are influenced by that structure of belief.

The whole of human life is in search of meaning and that meaning is a reflection of the state of consciousness, how they flow within the relative reality. Every individual has an idea of what they want in their life, a certain meaning to which they are devoted. Everyone is looking for their own version of sacred nature, for greatness within themselves. Our whole being is designed to evolve, our brains are designed to learn. We are capable of phenomenal creativity. Our bodies are capable of generating incredible, transcendental experiences. We are all looking in our own way, trying to find happiness, trying to find meaning, trying to find a certain sense of self-worth. Everyone is looking, whether they are looking in a correct manner or an incorrect manner; whatever their nature is, that is what they will find. We choose the direction in which we flow. If we look to be influenced by cultural icons and celebrities, these will be our deities and cultural archetypes. To be noble is to be a soul realising its nature, gaining that nobility, moving in the direction of cosmic consciousness, not being born into nobility. So those who start to move in the direction of knowing, looking for self-realisation, the true spirit, move towards liberation. Whatever your consciousness state is, you create a god based on that. It is not the Divine that made man in its image; it is man who made the Divine in their image. There are those individuals who are confused by the teachings and become obsessed with self-punishment and self-hatred. This is a reflection of the ego. They misunderstand the intention of this spiritual practice and the transcendence of the body and turn it into hating the body, punishing the body. This self-punishment is punishment of the spirit. These misunderstandings happen at the level of faith because if there is no knowing, then after a while faith leads one to conflict.

What you eat, you become. Your body takes on the value of what you put into it; it is the quality of the food that is important not just on the nutritional level but also vibrationally. The point of blessing one's food, being in gratitude for it, is to raise the vibrational quality of what you are consuming. By using the power of your sound and your intention, you uplift the vibrational quality of the food that you are consuming. That food promotes intelligence, vitality, cheerfulness; the fresher and more alive it is, the more energy there is. When we ingest pain into our system, when we consume it, it is bound to create disease physically and mentally within us. Increasing the quality, the higher energy, in our food can only improve our health physically and mentally. Be intelligent, be wise, in all aspects of your life, honour your human life. This human incarnation is the vehicle to realisation; if you do not realise it here, you cannot realise it elsewhere.

Faith becomes a great ally as a precursor to the dawning of wisdom; one must have that level of trust, that faith within one's own practice to liberate oneself. Within the context of the practice, if there is no faith in it, then it cannot move in the direction of knowing. The belief within one's own practice, within one's own journey, is a very relevant and important aspect of moving in the direction of knowing. If one doesn't have that belief, if one is moving with doubt, then it leads nowhere. This is a manual for evolution: how to behave, how to live, even how to eat, a full manual for life, how to live an elegant life of bliss. These teachings are a spiritual science which includes faith, includes love, a complete integrated way of being. But it is not the path, it is the one who is walking it who is the path. You are the path; the path is you.

Lesson 18
On Understanding the Meaning through Knowing the Meaninglessness

There are different aspects or stages of an individual's life. Firstly, dedication to realisation, laying down the strong foundation of a spiritual life for an integrated human being to live as an enlightened being. Then one gains a natural ability to engage in the relative field of reality as a conscious agent of evolution and be a part of the great Leela as a conscious leader for the betterment of the collective. Then, in the great scheme of nature, one realises how insignificant all the human systems are. So after one has played certain roles here, it is time to disengage, to un-identify, to journey away from the structures of society, from where interaction between fellow human beings happens, and return back to the deep silence; that natural letting go of all the roles, retreating into the arms of that great beloved, death. These are just stages of development depending on the evolution of the soul.

When one is fully established within oneself, then one is able to see simultaneously the meaning of it all while being profoundly aware of the absolute meaninglessness of it all. Then one becomes detached and one can be born into the state of integration that naturally starts to emerge. One can only achieve this when one has an internal state of bliss; bliss consciousness is there after renouncing, detaching and abandoning the fruits. It's the fire that burns, that illuminates, that purifies, that clears away the dust of ignorance that has gathered upon the consciousness field of the soul. As that fire is lit through that inner practice, one finds liberation. Without the journey through that fire, without going within oneself, there is no bliss; without bliss, there is no capacity to rise up from the field of relative reality. One remains entangled because one doesn't know bliss. As one naturally expands one's consciousness state, bliss is born.

The spiritual practice is an inner practice; it is dynamic, one cannot abandon it. One must continue to be compassionate, to serve and uplift. One must act, one must fulfil the need of the hour for we are instruments of the cosmic consciousness. That is the natural progression of the soul. This perceived boundary of an isolated self disappears; our nervous system becomes connected to the cosmic nervous system and the message becomes very clear. Spontaneous right action naturally arises while relinquishing the attachment to the result of that action. That is the quality of the individual who is awakening to their inner bliss nature. If you find the world to be unbearable, then you can never be free from it and you can never positively change it. If the driving force is trying to escape something, one will not find escape possible. For the world is a generator of experience. That's what the field does and the subjective interpretation of that experience is the duty of the knower of the field, not the field. So if the knower of the field wants to run away from the field purely because they find the field unbearable, it has nothing to do with the field itself. It has to do with the knower of the field and since that is the case, no matter where the knower goes, they cannot escape. Eventually the value of Self will catch up. We cannot escape ourself.

So the only way out is in. By consistently maintaining that inner practice, innocently engaging in the relative field of reality, one naturally develops the ability to be with what is. Then one elegantly fulfils the need of the hour while remaining unattached. Those who give up that inner practice out of fear, self-centeredness, not developing their own inner nature, do not find that freedom from bondage and the existential burden, that bliss that is the fruit. Brilliance cannot be born if one is attached to the result and one cannot be present if one doesn't have access to that inner awareness. That inner state of equanimity, that state of bliss, naturally makes one available to remaining and acting in a present manner, fulfilling the need of the hour. People who have a deep inner practice have that inner equanimous, fulfilled state. They come together with a shared vision, a shared intention without a particular attachment, without any agenda to find a greater happiness somewhere in the future. The kind of people you want to be among work to elevate society, elevate any environment they are in. People who have this kind of consciousness, whether working individually or together, raise up the whole status of the collective. They're not chasing something other, trying to manipulate the outcome and control everything. The wise know the futility of trying to take control.

The one who is moving in the direction of cosmic consciousness, rising above the lower mind, is discovering that inner equanimity, that inner presence, that inner bliss consciousness. That is a being who is naturally discovering love. Their heart is filling with love for the heart can only be filled with love from inside; it doesn't get filled from the outside. The most important things in your life all come from within. As one dives deep within oneself, love rises up and love knows only one thing, that is to love. Love is always loving, there is no effort in that. Love which is on the level of ego is tiring. To love oneself on the level of thought, that is exhausting because every second thought is of self-hatred; 'I must love myself', then you forget and start hating yourself again. But the love which is discovered is effortless; love filling up the heart from the inside, infused with cosmic intelligence, is the true bliss. Then one can live in a much more celebratory, blissed out, liberated manner. One can live from an intuitive place and experience the universe not as an enemy but as an ally. That is the nature of pure bliss.

In any action that one does, there is collaboration; no action occurs alone, the spirit has to collaborate. The cosmic spirit, the elements, the senses, all have to come together in collaboration for any action, any experience, to be possible in the relative field of reality. As long as there is any level of relativity in existence, there is activity. That activity is inherent in nature. It is not just in the individual; the activity of consciousness is the relative reality. So on the level of the localised value of Self, the soul, there are three aspects to the experience: the knower, the known and the process of knowing, supported by the relative field of reality. These aspects are behind all action and behind action there is knowledge; all action arises from knowledge and the origin of action is in thought. For the one diving deep within and simultaneously refining their intellect, their perception as the perceiver, unity in diversity and diversity in unity is being experienced. It is a holistic understanding, an integrated approach, not a reductionist one. Knowledge has to have that liberating quality to it; knowledge which is just on the surface does not liberate the knower. True knowingness liberates the knower.

Living is to be enjoyed, that is why we are here, but somehow, we become exhausted by it. It's a strange dilemma. The only thing we will all know is life, all this beauty and love, and yet somehow human beings find themselves exhausted by life itself. We try to create the life we want but end up creating chaos and then we find ourselves enslaved by our own creation. One builds a business, then one finds one cannot be at peace because of the business. One rises up to the status of leader but then finds the demands of leadership destroy one's sanity. The action which has no underlying experience of unity is an action which is dominated by stress and struggle, for action itself is not liberating, it is just mindless activity. Life without consistent refinement, without the cultivation of awareness, means the individual is not even aware of what they are doing most of the time. Of course, as I have said, in any moment of one's life, the dominant mode can change and become subservient and then it will change again. But action arises from the individual, so the consciousness state of that individual will dictate the nature of the action.

To raise one's level of supreme knowledge and joy, one has to establish oneself in a consistent practice, master the mind, master the energy, master the senses, refine the mind, refine the energy, refine the senses, and work within the field of energy. The one who is evolving is the one who is working with one's self, refining the self through the integrated approach, through consistent practice. Refining the functions of the mind, of the body, of the senses and raising the energy so that on every level the celestial value can be expressed. Whenever you are about to create some progressive change, that is when the resistance is at its strongest; you have to face the resistance of your own mind and body because there is a certain attachment to remaining the same. But for one to want to remain the same and to keep engaging in a certain way of living, it has to make sense, so it has to somehow generate the illusion of happiness on a certain level. One of the qualities of ignorance is to confuse unhappiness with happiness. The cosmic level of joy is born from within the individual out of their inner journey, their spiritual journey; it is born out of the refinement of the self. That is the joy born out of one's spiritual evolution, one's introspection and contemplation. But be aware, for in the beginning when one dives deep within oneself, one has to face the shadows; so it may feel like poison but it delivers the nectar. One has to realise that the truth can be scary depending on one's own evolutionary state. One may start to see things that one might be ignoring but ultimately, it will liberate. One has to go through the fire to turn into gold; the poison will gain the supreme nectar. This is the joy born out of one's spiritual quest, the true hero's journey, self-realisation. One cannot just believe in this joy; one has to experience it.

So ignorance, action and supreme joy are all available to us but the pleasures of constant action will not sustain you. There is nothing wrong with pleasure, pleasure is pleasing but without the backing of that supreme wisdom, that pleasure leads to misery. Ignorant joy is based in self-destruction and the destruction of others. When the individual is bound by that frequency, then they find joy only in those activities which destroy themselves or others. The supreme joy is not a belief; it is an experience. It is not a quick fix. It is a state that one reaches where the wisdom which is acquired liberates the individual from the lower tendencies. Joy born out of the realisation of sacredness, born out of the Divine, is that inherent joy within the silence of the being which rises up as the cosmic energy and starts to dance within us. But you will not just be in supreme joy once you drop the body. If you want to experience your own true nature, you have to begin now, for anything that exists now, exists then. The action backed by wisdom is itself nourishing and liberating. It is not the fruit at the end of the action but the action itself that is liberating.

All modes of behaviour, all the roles, have a certain quality. Whether you are a mother, a father, a student, a leader of an organisation or a musician, the roles are changing; you are never just one thing. You play different roles and you can bring that higher value to any role you play. Then you can raise the status of that whole activity, raise the status of what happens through you. When you show up, when you learn to serve, that is a divine life. When I was much younger, I lived in an ashram and there were many different jobs to do, very menial work like washing toilets, cleaning rooms, doing the gardens. In the beginning I had to get through my resistance but then it became a profoundly liberating journey. One of the masters who moved me deeply when I was there was this great Swami, an older man in his seventies. His job was to sweep the ashram. I didn't know when I first saw him, sweeping and singing away, how scholarly he was; I thought he was a cleaner but this man had a brilliant mind. He was very eloquent and learned yet there he was sweeping and chanting in such bliss; I had tears rolling down my face because he was in such bliss. He was playing the role of a cleaner, just sweeping the ashram, yet he was able to find that beauty, that divinity, in the simplest of actions. That is progression, the evolution of the self, to be that humble servant, that divine servant, for all true leaders are serving.

The way to victory is not to try to change others, not to try to control others, but is to apply oneself diligently to one's practice, to move in the direction of the Absolute, in the direction of the spirit, realising the sacred within and without. First, we build a strong foundation, transforming our own consciousness, our own being, then we taste victory, victory won through realisation. The supreme being dwells within the heart of every being irrespective of their belief system or status. These teachings cannot just be heard though; they have to be understood, embodied and contemplated. There has to be integration and practice; one has to dive deep within this ocean of wisdom. The listener gets to decide whether to understand that only those who are willing will realise and, in that realisation, they will gain liberation. Those who are not willing will not realise and that is OK too.

When this knowledge is embodied, it liberates the heart, it liberates the intellect, it liberates the soul. But it is up to the individual to choose whether to take the action. This is the beauty of these teachings; there is no coercion, only an invitation. This is an invitation of love. We have to choose to make the commitment because if we do this just as a mechanical act, it will make no difference. The world won't become a better place, our lives won't become better. No, we have to listen, learn and contemplate, then dive deep and embody it. But there is no judgement about what choice is made because everybody has the right to be right. We can choose to do whatever charms us. This love for us is unconditional and forever. This love is always there and available whether we dedicate ourself to realising our true Self or not. The love cannot stop loving anyone. The infinite cannot forsake the finite, for only the infinite exists. That supreme being, that one consciousness cannot forsake. If we take action, we will face the challenges that we have to face because nature will propel us to face that which we need to face. But all problems will be dissolved as we embody and practise these teachings. As we realise the truth, all misery will be resolved, all struggle will be dissolved. We will be strengthened by the light of wisdom and set free by this divine knowledge, for when we relinquish control and surrender there is only the opportunity to evolve, to grow.

These teachings will not be understood by those who do not practise. If one approaches this as merely a scholarly work, then one will totally miss the whole point, for one has to be a practitioner to understand. One has to teach from inside the teachings, one cannot just come at it from the outside. So those who do not have a deep practice will not understand. One must practise, meditate and contemplate. It should never be taught to those who are not willing to hear. It should not be taught to those who are not interested. It must never be a forced conversion. Everyone who comes to these teachings should come out of their own volition, through their own deserving power, their own worthy inquiry. For individuals who come to this teaching through their own worthy inquiry already have the deserving power; the worthy inquiry is a deserving power. It is a mature soul who is ready; the teachings should not be shared with those who are not willing, who are not ready. Don't ever try to force it down anybody's throat. Honour only the worthy inquiry.

The inquiry itself is a practice. The inquiry itself requires a certain level of awakening. That inquiry is the most important practice. Nothing will be understood by those lacking in love and devotion because without devotion, without love, there is no knowledge. Without knowledge, there is no love. So this wisdom, this supreme knowledge, will not be understood by the one who is lacking in devotion, lacking in that state of reverence, who is not receiving from the deepest level within themself. And it should definitely not be shared with those who are only interested in debate or fault finding, rather than inquiry. The supreme being dwells within everyone and nobody is going to suffer just because they do not listen. They will have their own life based on their own choices created from their own consciousness state. But those who do study and embody and practise shall gain liberation while living here; they will live a life of enlightenment, a life of gradually unfolding enlightenment. Remember enlightenment is not the goal; it is a continuous unfolding.

Wherever there is a teacher and a deserving student, somebody who is interested, who is engaged, then there is going to be supreme liberation. Wherever there is an evolving student, there is going to be victory. There is going to be glory, abundance and unfailing wellbeing. Wellbeing will spread in them, around them, through them, and a life of supreme joy will be theirs. Wherever there is that timeless path and there is the timeless realiser of that path, wherever there is a source of these teachings and there is a sincere student, an invincibility that cannot be defeated will prevail. There is going to be fulfilment. There is going to be a life of divine realisation, a life of supreme value, a life of love, a life of enlightenment.

About the Author

Born and raised in Rishikesh, Anand Mehrotra was mentored by his Guru from childhood. He went on to teach students from across the world and developed Sattva Yoga, an integrated approach to yoga through which people of all backgrounds, cultures and experiences can discover and embrace their own true nature. He then established the leading yoga teacher training school, Sattva Yoga Academy, and created Sattva Connect, the online platform for teachings and classes.

In addition to being a Master Yogi, Anand set up the charitable initiatives, Kushi Charitable Society and Sattva Foundation. He has been featured in several documentaries including award-winning *The Highest Pass* and continues to lead transformational motorcycle journeys into the Himalayas. *18 Insights on Life* is his fourth book.

Stay Connected

📘 *Sattva Yoga*
@sattvayogaacademy

📷 *Anand Mehrotra*
@theanandmehrotra

Sattva Yoga Academy
@sattvayogaacademy

🌐 *Sattva Yoga Academy*
sattvayogaacademy.com

Printed in France by Amazon
Brétigny-sur-Orge, FR

15619587R00130